Covering Clinton

Covering Clinton

The President and the Press in the 1990s

Joseph Hayden

Praeger Series in Presidential Studies

Westport, Connecticut
London

U.S. CIP information is on file at the Library of Congress.

British Library Cataloguing in Publication Data is available.

ISBN: 0–275–97034–5
ISSN: 1062–0931

First published in 2002

Praeger Publishers, 88 Post Road West, Westport, CT 06881
An imprint of Greenwood Publishing Group, Inc.
www.praeger.com

Printed in the United States of America

The paper used in this book complies with the
Permanent Paper Standard issued by the National
Information Standards Organization (Z39.48–1984).

10 9 8 7 6 5 4 3 2 1

Contents

Acknowledgments

I would like to thank James Sabin of Greenwood Press for his belief in this project, as well as his steadfast encouragement along the way. At Greenwood, Jennifer Debo patiently answered all my questions, and Fran Lyons provided able editing advice.

The first chapter of this book began as a seminar paper I wrote in the early 1990s for the eccentric, Diet-Coke–drinking David Thelen at Indiana University. His early comments helped shape my thinking about the mixture of politics and the media. Two other IU professors deserve special thanks, too. George Juergens and David Nord, each in his own unique way, showed me that it is possible for terrific researchers to be wonderful teachers. Their tireless enthusiasm for journalism history inspired me to want to write this book in the first place.

I am grateful to my parents, Raymond and Violetta Hayden, for the lively discussions we have had over the years about presidents, the press, and politics generally. (Perhaps now is a good time to apologize to the rest of my family for having to endure those discussions.)

Finally, I want to thank my wife, Gloria, for seeing this through with me.

Introduction

I first became aware of Bill Clinton in the summer of 1988. That year, at the Democratic Convention in Atlanta, Clinton gave one of the all-time worst speeches in American political history. Much of the fault was not his, but due to noisy conventioneers and to distractions on the floor. Nonetheless, his reputation as a fast-rising Democratic star looked dubious. Three years later, Clinton announced his candidacy for president of the United States. Yet, within just a few months he became the subject of not one but three personal scandals. Though each story by itself appeared either trivial (what he had smoked, whom he had slept with) or no longer newsworthy (what he had done during the war), all the charges together spelled catastrophe for his campaign, and I remember wondering how on earth this guy from Arkansas expected to get into the White House when he couldn't give a speech and couldn't avoid winding up in supermarket tabloids. Did he have a media death wish?

But then Bill Clinton did something remarkable. He reached out to and captured a sizable part of the American electorate by using public forums that most politicians normally avoided. In a rapidly changing media market, this forty-six-year-old presidential hopeful courted talk shows and MTV, "town hall meetings," and the Fox network's *Arsenio Hall*. While the Washington press corps was focused on the scandals and on his political liabilities, Bill Clinton was convincing voters amid informal settings that he knew enough and would work hard enough to make a good president. In November, forty-four million people showed they believed in him—a testament to his successful campaign strategy, as well as to a solid understanding of the mass media in America in the 1990s.

This book widens the picture of Clinton's relationship with the mass media. I begin with the story of that improbable campaign run of '92, take a look at his first-term transition into the White House, examine his very different campaign experience in 1996, and then discuss the biggest crisis he faced in office—the scandal that led to his impeachment in 1998. I will address his weak but slowly improved record on First Amendment issues, then, finally, consider his penchant for inspiring dramatic interpretations of his presidency and for stimulating debates about his legacy. With both, it turns out, he has shown a powerful fascination.

Indeed, that fascination with the media and with image may itself be one of the hallmarks of Clinton's political style. Naturally, all politicians have to be concerned with how the public perceives them, and good democrats are supposed to listen to what the people want. Still, few presidents, including Ronald Reagan, have seemed so absorbed by polling, focus groups, Hollywood, and celebrity. Bill Clinton spent a lifetime learning how to be a likable political leader, and for the most part he succeeded in becoming one. In fact, if we've learned anything about Bill Clinton, it is that he adores popularity.

On the whole, however, his quest for political stardom came without the usual suspects: namely, journalists. Journalists proved politically sympathetic but occupationally antagonistic. One frequently hears the term "adversarial" used to describe the relationship between the president and the press, but in most cases neither one really adopts that attitude, because the more adversarial the press becomes, the more likely the president is to curtail contact. Likewise, the less friendly the White House becomes, the more likely the president is to receive "bad press." For any politician, the relationship is not normally adversarial, then, but more akin to a business alliance with a natural predator. When the latter smells weakness, incompetence, wrongdoing, or scandal—when the press otherwise begins to lose respect for an administration—the relationship can become somewhat adversarial, as it did at times, say, during the Johnson and Nixon administrations.

This book is about the president and the press, but it should be noted that when I refer to "the press" I am talking about much more than simply newspapering, and so I use the terms "press" and "media" interchangeably. I am including television news and the worlds of punditry and talk shows, because journalism today has rapidly expanded into entertainment in much the same fashion that politics has seeped into show business, a merger that helps to explain the fluctuating political fortunes of William Jefferson Clinton.

1

The Empathy Candidate and the Living Room Campaign

INTRODUCTION

In 1992, Bill Clinton appeared on numerous television talk shows to explain why he wanted to be president. But he was not the only campaigning politician to choose such programming. In fact, most of the presidential contenders were also regularly scheduling and considering them, and Americans were watching the presidential campaign with unusually keen interest, no doubt in part because candidate after candidate resorted to such unconventional forums. Politicians' use of them seemed new and exciting at the time, and throughout the year this phenomenon sparked questions which most of us only half-attempted to answer or even think about. What we were observing was presently happening, after all, and it is often difficult to make sense of events without some measure of hindsight. The questions, though, were easy to identify. Would these politicians encounter problems and distractions in pushing an agenda via such media? Might they suffer embarrassments?

Before the primary season began, talk show host Dennis Miller had asked vice presidential candidate Al Gore whether he or his wife, Tipper, rolled the tighter joint. Gore was neither prepared for the question, nor pleased with the laughter that ensued. Could a politician preserve the "dignity" of the process and of the office he hoped to win? What was this dignity? What would happen to the role traditionally played by the national press corps, the who's who of the giant dailies and TV networks? Did we really need the stuffy Morton Deans, David Broders, Robert MacNeils, and Bob Woodwards anyway? And what about that oddball population of policy wonks, think-tankers, political consultants, and academics who are cloyingly summoned to the pages of newspapers and magazines and to broadcast programming to provide us with instant "expert" opinion and insight? Does democracy lose or gain by the addition of less-serious, or at least less-credentialed or less-professional, mediators? Finally, how would the public react to politicians circumventing normal media channels? Would voters obtain adequate information or have to settle for serenades of schmooze and schmaltz? Would they even care? My understanding of these issues has benefitted from the perspective of a variety of journalists and scholars who have reflected on the "new media," as well as a wide reading of the news that both candidates and the media made during that period. But what are these "new media"?

They weren't new in 1992, nor was their use unprecedented, but the extent, the prominence, and the impact of their political use were. The new media included toll-free telephone numbers, satellite linkups, "town meetings," video production and distribution, cable television, and above all the television talk show (to which I pay particular attention here)—communications formats and programming providing political candidates with freer, more direct access to the public. What these forums shared was a striking tendency to eliminate the middleman, the journalist, and so to close the distance between voter and candidate. In a subtle way, they seemed almost to apologize for the necessity of the mass media themselves. How and why did the use of the so-called new media become so prevalent in 1992? Did Bill Clinton pave the way for their use? How did both the "old" and the "new" journalists view their roles, and what did they think they and their competitors were doing?

In all these sources, there is a discernible effort to give the emergence of the new media increasingly serious attention during the course of the campaign. Originally, I thought criticism was more favorable toward the end of the year, but the evidence has not quite borne this out. A number of articles appeared early in the campaign that do praise the existence of more forums, if not specific uses of them. And even a couple of old network news dogs found something commendable in the newer media. So the story of the '92 campaign is a more complicated tale than that of the mainstream political press first laughing off the newcomers, then gradually accepting them. The newcomers did, however, firmly impress themselves on the minds of journalists and students of journalism. A strangely transformed communications landscape constituted the singular theme everyone surveyed in this chapter remembers as best capsulating the presidential politics of that year, a remarkable time generally for the mass media in America. "Teledemocracy," "direct-access politics," and "call-in candidacy" are just a few of the buzzwords and phrases which have entered the lexicon in our fast-forming mythology surrounding the 1992 campaign. And Bill Clinton, it is safe to say, played a large role in highlighting and exploiting, if not quite creating, those changes. Here, indeed, was a very different sort of political candidate.

THE EMPATHY CANDIDATE

Payoff

Washington, D.C., was clear, cool, and sunny, on January 20, 1993, ideal weather for drawing a large, spirited crowd for the inauguration of William Jefferson Clinton. And hundreds of thousands of people did come to watch—some to witness America's routine changing of the guard, others to behold a more interesting generational change in the country's leadership, still others for predictable political reasons. But the joy evident on many faces impressed a number of reporters. "Cheerful chaos reigned in the streets," one newspaper correspondent noted.[1] It was indeed a festive mood that people exhibited, an elation suggestive of a sort of Woodstock for older, more affluent folks.

Just before noon, Chief Justice William Rehnquist asked the former governor of Arkansas to raise his right hand and pledge to uphold and faithfully execute the laws of the United States to the best of his ability. With his wife and daughter by his side, Clinton did so promise, and within minutes was duly sworn in as America's 42nd president. Nothing unusual. A routine political moment accompanied by the usual solemnity. But writers have always noted the quiet beauty of Washington's inaugural ceremonies, which constitute, certainly, a grand event, the closest thing in a republic approaching the dignity and glamor of other countries' royal pageantry. Even veteran reporters enjoyed themselves. "You had to be a committed naysayer not to be caught up in the significance of the occasion, the exhilaration of the crowd, the honest high spirits," one correspondent observed.[2]

Still, this president's inauguration seemed to offer something more. One important dimension was the jubilation of a political party and its supporters which had won the presidency only half as many times as the opposition since the end of World War II, the last occasion being Jimmy Carter's electoral squeaker in 1976. But the nostalgic revisiting of a sixteen-year memory accounted for only a part of the inauguration's special tenor. The atmosphere in Washington that day also reflected the philosophy of the postwar Democratic Party, which since Lyndon Johnson had declared its determination to embrace the causes of common people, including, especially, women and minorities. The belief that the party of "the people," as opposed to the party of privilege, had triumphed in the election lent almost a sense of indignation to the joyousness apparent on the scene. As one bewitched bystander exclaimed, "I haven't slept. I'm punch drunk. . . . I just feel like I'm in this place called Clinton-land." The fact that the spectator, Karen Russell, was an agent for the film industry did not diminish her faith in her party's inclusiveness: "I thought I was a jaded Hollywood person, but to see a President take an oath and the next person to speak is a black woman in the white guy's club is amazing."[3]

Yet, perhaps the most striking element in the day's exultation was the simple fact that Bill Clinton had beaten the odds, for many celebrants a deeply satisfying knowledge mixed with the sweet sense of revenge. Here too was a storyteller's dream: the dramatic, even inspiring, comeback story about a down-and-outer who refused to quit and won it all. Clinton, we must remember, was a virtual unknown at the beginning of 1992, and yet the better known he became the more beleaguered he was, because Clinton was not just an underdog but an unlikely candidate with serious liabilities. To be sure, the Arkansas contender sported promising abilities and an encouraging gubernatorial record, but he was also a man with worrisome personal traits and several gaping political vulnerabilities—vulnerabilities so manifest that most pundits were quick to write him off at the outset of the campaign.

Political Baggage

Clinton had evaded the Vietnam War draft in the 1960s. Instead of complying with conscription when his number came up, he sought an exemption and used every contact he could think of to obtain one. Clinton's attempt to avoid the draft was hardly exceptional among college students. As James Fallows has written, many young men of that generation first tried a graduate school deferment, then getting into the National Guard, and if that failed, a medical excuse: "Some students noticed their asthma getting worse, others had trick knees. I lost ten pounds and became too skinny to be 1-A."[4] Clinton was not exactly honorable in staying out of the draft, however. Upon his release from duty, he returned to Oxford University instead of the Arkansas National Guard, as he had apparently promised and for which he was spared from the army in the first place. Eluding military service during the Vietnam War was, of course, not news then or even two decades later, but Clinton's dishonesty about the details of his past was. He told the press a year before the election that he had always wanted to serve in the armed forces.[5] In 1992, he denied ever having received an induction notice, having had someone pull strings on his behalf, and having even opposed the draft itself. But when reporters found evidence to the contrary, including Clinton's original correspondence with ROTC commander Eugene Holmes and archival records from Senator William Fullbright's office, Clinton had to retract one statement after another.[6]

Clinton was similarly untruthful in answering early questions about his experience using marijuana. At first he said he didn't, then he said he did but didn't inhale, a hilarious excuse which embarrassed even his supporters. By lying, Clinton was doing something that legal writer Alan Dershowitz would later, in the Monica Lewinsky scandal, judge to be among the president's worst faults: attempting to gain some short-term political ground regardless of the long-term consequences.[7] Yet, even in the short term, Clinton paid a price. The continual need for the awkward revision of previous statements brought him ridicule, and in New York in April, Clinton finally lashed out at a derisive citizen, complaining bitterly about "all this crap I've put up with for the last six months."[8] Columnist Roger Simon expressed skepticism then that Clinton could last long in such a firestorm: "Bill Clinton thinks that he is going through the tough part of the campaign. . . . But Clinton is wrong. Because wait until he gets to the general election and faces George Bush. And wait until George Bush gets asked if he ever used marijuana. And Bush replies, 'No, when I was that age, I was in the Pacific fighting for my country.' See what I mean, Bill? This is the *easy* part."[9]

The third of Clinton's triumvirate of vulnerabilities was his penchant for adulterous affairs and, still more, his lying about them. In 1992, an Arkansas lounge singer named Gennifer Flowers held a press conference to tell the world that for more than a decade she had been the governor's lover. Clinton denied any intimate relationship, even though Flowers played a tape-recorded phone message between the two, which clearly indicated that she, not he, was telling the truth. Clinton could not have incurred any more obvious strikes against his candidacy.

The Clinton Campaign Team

Facing this army of political skeletons was a youthful but surprisingly experienced staff of dedicated political advisors. James Carville headed the campaign team. The forty-seven-year-old strategist, sloganeer, and media ham enjoyed showcasing his quick wit and zestful personality, but he was a chief aide of real substance, someone with limitless energy and reliable political instincts. Carville could analyze a problem and rapidly come up with several possible solutions to it. The Ragin' Cajun, as he was known, loved his job, and it showed. He dominated campaign strategy by force of personality alone, a personality infused with the image he carefully cultivated—that of a "common man in uncommon surroundings." David Von Drehle described him as having the "unsettling look of a man who might, without much warning, hole up in the woods with an arsenal of guns and a supply of canned food."[10] Carville was a story all by himself, and not coincidentally, a media darling.

Indeed, in one of the stranger coincidences of the campaign—an almost implausible plotline—Carville was dating one of George Bush's key advisers, Mary Matalin, a woman he would eventually marry. The two rivals actually shared much in common, some journalists noted at the time: "Each is the closest thing either campaign has to someone with street smarts. Just as Matalin is politically more liberal than Bush, Carville is more conservative than Clinton. Both are up-by-the-bootstraps white ethnics whose rough-cut personalities don't always fit neatly in a business that has been dominated by slick schmoozers."[11] The Carville-Matalin romance gave color to the campaign and lent a bemused affection for the people behind the scenes. But above all it was Carville himself who smoothed relations between the media, particularly the more established figures in it, and candidate Clinton. Carville's self-conscious drawl and his relentless sense of humor proved irresistible to journalists, who found him endlessly entertaining and likable, as well as informed, crudely opinionated, and insightful.

Carville's partner was George Stephanopoulos, thirty-one years old, and certainly the youngest-looking member of the Clinton team. Looks were deceiving, however, for the native New Yorker was an unusually bright and resourceful strategist with impressive experience. Stephanopoulos manned what came to be known as "the war room," an operations center responsible for combatting every attack sent their way the second it came out, even, in fact, anticipating likely attacks and squashing them before they did emerge. As Stephanopoulos later described their function, "In the end, a political campaign boils down to talk, talk, and more talk. What are they saying? What are we saying? What are they saying about what we're saying in response to your question? And on and on and on."[12] By fax, phone, or regular mail, then, Clinton's staff was prepared to send volleys of propaganda to any journalist or opinion-maker in America. The war room, in essence, was the campaign's general headquarters for handling the mainstream press, and its military motif was certainly emblematic of Clinton's overall attitude toward older, conventional media, to the Washington press corps, in particular.

The mastermind behind Clinton's appearances on new-media venues was thirty-four-year-old media consultant Mandy Grunwald, daughter of media scion Henry Grunwald, once the editor in chief of *Time* magazine. Mandy Grunwald was a Harvard graduate who had already worked for U.S. senators like Daniel Patrick Moynihan, Wendell Ford, and Patrick Leahy. Despite her eventual preference for alternative media, Grunwald could carry herself, and Bill Clinton, rather well in dealing with established media programs. In January 1992, while responding to questions about Gennifer Flowers, for example, Grunwald acquitted herself so well during a joint appearance with Clinton on the American Broadcasting Company's (ABC's) late-night program *Nightline*, even Ted Koppel was forced to admit on air that she had "done a very effective job of putting me on the defensive."[13]

Clinton and the New Media

Nonetheless, it was precisely those respected programs like *Nightline* that pushed Grunwald to look elsewhere for her boss to make his case to the American people. Mainstream reporters, she felt, were fixated on scandals, crises, and controversies. They seemed more interested in Clinton's reaction to questions about past embarrassments than they were in his ideas for future policies—his perspective on issues concerning the economy, health care, or Social Security. Old-style reporters wouldn't let him move beyond his less-than-sublime personal history. In fact, journalists were so preoccupied with confronting Clinton about his controversial past that they often failed to observe one of his most impressive qualities on display in the present: a solicitous, reassuring compassion.

At one campaign stop, he hugged a woman on the verge of tears because she couldn't afford medical care. "I think he's the smartest guy I've ever met," Clinton's adviser Paul Begala reflected. "But his most compelling attribute is that interpersonal empathy. When he is connecting with someone, the whole world melts away."[14]

Grunwald's challenge, therefore, was to avoid confrontations seeking the governor's apology or defensive reaction, and instead to find forums where he might showcase his gift for more pleasant conversation. The key, she believed, was finding opportunities for Clinton to speak at leisure and at length, so Grunwald sought out television programs with more amicable hosts, more flexible or informal settings, and with younger audiences. By the summer, he was fully immersed in doing so, appearing on the *Arsenio Hall Show*, MTV, *Donahue*, and *Larry King Live*. Clinton, the "empathy candidate," thrived in these arenas. For reasons that can best be summed up in the succinct phrase that he was "good with people," Clinton had obviously found an environment in which to put his interpersonal skills to work. But these environments were uniquely and inherently structured to do that for any candidate, which is why so many other office seekers quickly turned to them as well.

A question and answer session on MTV, for example, juxtaposed a presidential candidate with a group of young, star-struck people, many of whom scarcely exhibited a sophisticated knowledge of current events or issues. A striking number of the young questioners, in fact, acted like giddy fans in the presence of one of the program's unplugged musicians. In addition to the innocuous quality of the audience, a group one journalist likened to "churchgoers," the MTV program offered Clinton maximum opportunity to express himself uninterrupted and with little serious cross-examination.[15] This was obviously not *Meet the Press*, where guests are confronted by interrogating journalists.

But it would be a mistake to conclude that a program like MTV's *Facing the Future with Bill Clinton* was less informative than one like *Meet the Press*, for it was informative in different ways. The point is that candidates rightly viewed the former as friendlier and freer. They could anticipate being able to get across a particular message or set of messages without fierce objection, sarcasm, or incredulity. Such a format provided them with considerable latitude. And for Clinton, who was spending valuable time combatting rearguard scandal-mongers, these programs were a vital and welcoming departure. One Democratic fundraiser in California introduced Clinton by saying that there had "never been a candidate who's more substantively talked about what he plans to do as President."[16] Regardless of the historical accuracy of that claim, Clinton was able to talk so substantively in 1992 precisely because of heretofore unutilized forums like cable television entertainment programming.

From Clinton's perspective, the highlight of the new-media experience in the 1992 campaign was undoubtedly the series of formal debates between the candidates. Not ostensibly new or novel, these forums confirmed the triumph of Clinton's campaign style when he got up out of his chair, strolled toward the audience, and confidently fielded questions. He then proceeded to engage in a bit of give-and-take with the audience, saying the right things, using the right gestures, expressing an appealing and authentic-sounding empathy for the voters in the crowd. "I feel your pain" became the famous mantra associated with Bill Clinton's campaign style. Compared to the more sedentary candidate Ross Perot and the quintessentially self-contained George Bush, Bill Clinton shone as a master of personable political acumen.

When Ross Perot spoke on *Larry King Live* in early 1992, he started what would become the most significant political trend of the year, the gravitation toward unconventional forums for political discussion and imagery. But if Perot launched the new movement, no one better personified it or excelled at it than Bill Clinton. Candidate Clinton was simply a natural. Better than any contender for political office since John F. Kennedy at combining an impressive mastery of the issues and a quick grasp of public relations fundamentals, Clinton fused the instincts of a policy wonk with the ploys of a seasoned actor. He knew what "played well" and appealed to most Americans. Part of that insight was the result of his religious reliance on public opinion polling, but much of it was also due to his quite extraordinary personal gifts (his ability to convey sincerity, compassion, and earnestness), as well as to the generation from which he sprang.

Clinton is a baby boomer, the nation's first to become president. He had grown up with television; he hadn't looked on warily or dismissively or uncertainly as television grew up. Therefore, he understood in a visceral way the demands of the medium, and the importance of being photogenic. Aides naturally advised him on what to do and say—that's their job—but no one had to tell Clinton, as consultants had to tell George Bush, how crucial it was to impart the right impression to viewers. And that's really the crux of the difference between the two men: Clinton knew that in an electronic age, voters were by definition *viewers*. Bush had to be reminded of that. Furthermore, Clinton's staff did not have to micromanage their boss's appearances. They trusted him to smile and wave, laugh and charm, mug and mingle. Clinton was like Lyndon Johnson without the hard edges. He depended on his attractive, engaging personal manner, his likeability, to win support. The editorial writer Edwin Yoder described Clinton's talent well in distinguishing him from another famous southern governor, Jimmy Carter: "Mr. Clinton is a political man. He knows that politics is a vital and complex art; and that its traditional techniques of bargaining, fraternizing and compromise— all of which Mr. Carter found distasteful—are essential."[17] Of the three techniques, fraternizing was clearly Clinton's favorite tactic and best-developed forté. According to a 1996 study of presidential personalities designed by psychological researchers, Clinton ranked third in extroversion—the quality of being outgoing, sociable, friendly—coming in just behind Theodore and Franklin Roosevelt.[18] Indeed, that study, in which dozens of historians participated, concluded that America's 42nd president was a lot like its 37th and its 7th, Lyndon Johnson and Andrew Jackson: " 'good ol' boys' who get low marks for character and integrity but rank high in the need for excitement and in their creative leadership style."[19]

Clinton's affinity for stimulating new forums thus capitalized on his foremost personal strengths. He pushed the boundaries of political television both because he was uniquely capable of it and because he had no other choice if he wanted to win. Clinton personified and best exploited the untapped possibilities of electronic electioneering, proving in the process that staid press conferences and intensely high-pressure tête-à-têtes with journalists were neither the only way to communicate to and through the media, nor necessarily the best way. Bill Clinton rose to power in 1992 on the back of the new media, television talk shows in particular, but his victory was also a story about seemingly new methods. What Clinton realized in 1992 was that soft-news exposure was just as helpful to his campaign as hard-news exposure; that being seen and heard were more important than being written about; and that televised contact with ordinary voters in low-key situations was more profitable than regular meetings with "professional" journalists. Communing with the public was the desired objective, and if some of the people had nonpolitical questions to ask, so much the better.

Clinton's exploitation of the new media had not come serendipitously in 1992. As governor of Arkansas, he had grown wary of conventional news organizations, especially after losing reelection in 1980, and so experimented with alternative media in subsequent races. David Maraniss has pointed out in his biography, *First in His Class*, that Clinton preferred using the "paid media" (commercials and mailings) during the 1980s, and "flanking the press" in the process, as longtime consultant Dick Morris put it.[20] Bill Clinton liked being in control of public appearances, a freedom obviously curtailed by the presence of straight-news reporters. He also preferred not to share the spotlight, and the correspondents of major media organizations are nothing if not stage-friendly. Even in Arkansas, finding alternatives to the capital press corps proved more reliable than surrendering to the whims of journalists hungry for scoops. At any rate, Clinton thrived in low-key and informal settings.

Toward the end of that decade, the lesson was brought home with particular force. In 1988, four years before running for president of the United States, the forty-two-year-old governor of Arkansas appeared on the National Broadcasting Company's (NBC's) *Tonight Show*. Clinton badly needed the positive exposure. Days earlier, he had embarrassed himself at the Democratic National Convention with a speech that ran on far too long and that was mainly inaudible because of distraction and noise on the convention floor. Cameras there had shown the delegates' indifference, with one man clearly seen giving the governor the hook sign to stop speaking. Overnight, Clinton had become a national joke, trapped in the image of a droning politician who talked rather than listened and who didn't know when enough was enough. Clinton's friend and television producer Harry Thomason helped arrange the appearance on the *Tonight Show* to counter the ridicule the governor was receiving in the press and on television. Before a quieter, captive audience, Clinton played the saxophone and made small talk with host Johnny Carson, and all in all the event went well. Clinton demonstrated his good-natured humor, but also his resiliency and determination to control what others thought of him. Considering the fact that pundits had all but pronounced Clinton's political future washed up, the *Tonight Show* appearance signaled an encouraging recovery, and, in retrospect, the beginning of something new.

THE NEW MEDIA

Television's Year

The year 1992 was a fitting time for "the talk show campaign" because it was an extraordinary year for television, and for NBC in particular.

The network was losing two enormously popular sitcoms, *Cheers* and the *Cosby Show*, and also bidding farewell to one of its oldest employees. After thirty years as host of the *Tonight Show*, Johnny Carson announced he would air his last program on May 22. The media's nostalgic countdown to that date and the stampede of celebrities avid to share the spotlight with Carson occasioned a spate of news stories, features, and columns so voluminous that by one measure Carson ended up receiving more press that year than presidential candidate Jerry Brown.[21] The following *USA Today* reference, only one of hundreds, is not atypical of the tone used by many publications: "Johnny, it's not that we hardly knew ye, but we probably knew ye too well. Even took you for granted."[22] Carson, another writer insisted, had been "the barometer of the nation."[23] The panegyrics continued unabated into the next year.

While journalists got misty-eyed about Carson's imminent departure, NBC executives were counting on another public relations boon in planning something unique for that quadrennial orgy of athletics known as the Olympics. Their weapon was a high-tech toy they dubbed the "triplecast"—satellite broadcasts of three distinctive kinds of Olympics coverage from Seoul, South Korea, from which prepaying viewers could select. It represented, appropriately enough, NBC's attempt to give Americans a choice in programming by letting them decide whether they wanted to watch basketball or wrestling, boxing or table tennis. It was also, of course, a means for the network to garner as large an audience as possible in order to make as much money from advertisers as it could. But the high cost of subscribing to any of the three services kept viewers away, and NBC lost millions of dollars by summer's end. The profitability of price-tag democracy proved elusive.

Perhaps democracy itself seemed elusive when Americans glimpsed arguably the most horrific thirty seconds of television that year: the beating by policemen of motorist Rodney King in Los Angeles. An amateur photographer videotaped that incident, an act that would have profound consequences for not just California but the entire country. Columnists and commentators across the nation condemned the arrest as a detestable example of police brutality. President Bush told reporters that the video sickened him. Blacks cited the event as a grim measure of how far they had yet to go to receive real justice in a predominantly white society. Weeks later, when a jury acquitted all four officers of wrongdoing, Los Angeles erupted in a series of riots. Residents vented their outrage over an ostensibly unfair verdict and a discriminatory criminal justice system by burning, looting, beating, and killing. Dozens of people died during the upheaval. In a matter of days, a substantial part of the city lay in ruin. One by one, presidential candidates, their staffs, and a trailing entourage of media personnel cautiously came to Los Angeles to investigate, consult, and pay their respects. Suddenly, but to no one's surprise, urban blight and the plight of the cities landed on the nation's political agenda again. Everyone was talking about the events in Los Angeles, and everyone's point of reference began with the grainy image of four cops cudgelling a black man into unconsciousness.

Television included the bizarre, too, and for our purposes, a very relevant connection between Hollywood and politics. Vice president Quayle had become embroiled in this mix in the summer of 1992, during a campaign speech trumpeting his vision of "family values" and decrying their apparent meaninglessness to "the media elite," and to television in particular. He mentioned by name the fictional character Murphy Brown (from the sitcom of the same name) as an example of a deviant role model—a single mother—who appeared not to suffer much from her lack of a man and who appeared to be portraying a fatherless family as an acceptable norm. For the next few months, the show's star, Candace Bergen, and producer, Linda Bloodworth-Thomason, exchanged salvos with Quayle, incorporating his comments into the season opener, along with a bristling retort: "We've had enough discussion about family values. It's time to pass some legislation that values families."[24] Bush got burned worse. After he singled out the much-extinct TV series *The Waltons* for its inspiring ideal of family life, one, he said, superior to that depicted on *The Simpsons*, Bart Simpson complicated the comparison: "We're just like the Waltons. We're praying for the Depression to end, too."[25] Sitcoms, it seemed, enjoyed talk of politics, even if they did not always match the satirical flair of *The Simpsons*. Throughout 1992, politics was indeed alive and well on television, and you didn't have to turn to public television, network news, or even the Cable News Network (CNN) to get it.

Perot and the Coming of the Talk Shows

Although most people today remember Bill Clinton as the pioneer of new media political campaigning, it was not actually Clinton but H. Ross Perot who first capitalized on alternative forums. On February 20, 1992, Perot appeared on CNN's *Larry King Live* and flatly told the host he would not run for president that year, saying he did not like the present

political system and insisting that he could make a more effective contribution to the country from outside the White House. Besides, he did
not think he was "temperamentally fit" for the job. Perot and King then
chatted for sixty minutes about a wide variety of topics—from the presidential candidates to America's foreign competitors—but mostly ad-
dressing economic issues such as how to create jobs yet still reverse the
nation's four-trillion-dollar debt in the midst of a recession. After the
second-to-last commercial break, a few minutes before the show's close,
King tried once more: "By the way, is there any scenario in which you
would run for President? Can you give me a scenario in which you'd
say, 'OK, I'm in'?" Perot squirmed and fidgeted, but finally conceded
that if volunteers managed to place his name on the ballot in all fifty
states, he would enter the race. "I am not encouraging people to do this
. . . but the push has to come from them."[26]

The encounter thrilled Larry King. He understood that Perot could
easily alter the course of the campaign if he joined the race, even though
he might not win. And King knew at once how important his own program had become, that it had played a critical role in accelerating the
announcement of Perot's candidacy, if not in launching it in the first
place:

I was excited. I don't know if I recognized at that moment how significant
Perot's promise to run was, but I knew there was a tremendous hunger for a
new candidate—someone else, *anyone* else to run. And I knew there was tremendous anger at Washington and its regular inhabitants. Perot seemed to have
the power to tap into both pools of public frustration. But I didn't know if he
could pull it off. What if he did? I felt like a cross between Dr. Frankenstein
and a Hollywood talent scout.[27]

Within a few hours, viewers besieged CNN's Atlanta switchboard to find
out how they could contact Perot. Within days, "his enthusiasts jammed
the phone lines at his businesses. Even unlisted numbers at his offices
rang off the hook."[28]

Yet, this phenomenon early in the year elicited little coverage or comment by the national press corps. For example, a news database (Nexis)
search of the *New York Times* and the *Washington Post* reveals no mention at all during the month of February of Perot's TV appearance and
his possible candidacy. A search of *all* news sources on the Nexis system
reveals just seventeen overall stories during that month, but fifteen of
these come from CNN itself! Of the other two, one is from a television

trade journal (*TV Monitor*), the other an anonymous dispatch the *Los Angeles Times* printed on page eighteen. Indeed, it was not until Perot's more formal June campaign, when he hired professional campaigners Hamilton Jordan and Edward Rollins, that reporters really paid attention and gave full publicity to the independent candidacy, by which time they had already begun to seem foolish and out of touch for ignoring it in the first place.

The other candidates had taken notice, however. Their staffs monitored Perot closely throughout the year and drew inspiration from his more successful tactics. Certain candidates, though, had little choice in courting new media. Jerry Brown's much-underfunded campaign needed cheaper sources of publicity than television advertisements, and Bill Clinton needed more favorable news coverage from reporters, who were regularly skewering him with their stories about his extramarital affairs and his evasion of the draft during the Vietnam War. Both candidates joined the talk show circuit, then, to secure a forum with which they could "get their message out" to the public and which they could use free of charge. Television programs such as *Donahue* and *Larry King Live*, ABC's *Good Morning America*, NBC's *Today*, and the Columbia Broadcasting System's *CBS This Morning* were popular choices. By the end of the campaign, Bush, Clinton, and Perot had appeared on those programs a combined one hundred times.[29] Bush and Clinton frequented radio talk shows, too, and made heavy use of local media in general. Of all the candidates, Clinton was probably best suited for these forums; he related well to ordinary people by asking *them* questions and then listening attentively to the responses.

No one else, though, enjoyed Ross Perot's level of influence or popularity. Talk shows wanted him badly because his presence guaranteed lavish ratings. As television journalist Sam Donaldson pointed out wryly, "it's a pretty pass. . . . Bill Clinton can only get on television and get noticed if he plays the saxophone with Arsenio Hall. George Bush holds a news conference—he can't get on television. Ross Perot can get on television any time he wants. What have we come to . . . ?"[30] Public disenchantment with politics as usual—and often with the usual candidates—the availability of alternative forums for more unusual candidates, plus Perot's special blend of informed patriotism and rocking-chair charisma gave the sixty-one-year-old Texan the leverage he needed to run an aggressive, effective campaign.

But Perot also tapped into a potent vein of media criticism shared by voters, candidates, and even the media themselves, which made him immediately credible and likeable to large numbers of people. Perot relished invoking the bugbear of the 1988 campaign, the candidates' ever-shrinking television news sound bite, whose average length that year was just nine seconds, a record low.[31] Journalists took a beating for it too, and, even by their own admission, fully deserved the reproach. Howard Kurtz describes the legacy of that campaign:

After the grand debacle of 1988, when the press felt used and manipulated by political consultants, journalists vowed at countless seminars and symposiums and in-house soul-searching sessions that they would change their ways. They would cover the issues. They would not do sleaze. They would not act as mind-less conduits for empty photo ops and 30-second smears. They would not be-come fixated on the horse race.[32]

Perot delighted in raising the sound bite issue, then, as a way of re-minding journalists that their traditional methods of news gathering sometimes failed and almost always invited scorn. "Let's not sound bite it," he was fond of saying, if not obeying. One newspaper writer ob-served bitterly that Perot seldom followed his own advice: He protested against the media's tendency to abbreviate people's comments, yet with-out fail, "he launches into a sound bite, often less than 30 seconds."[33] Indeed, a glance at the transcript of any Perot interview dependably shows a scarcity of sustained focus; Perot did change topics quickly. But whether the viewers noticed Perot's transgressions, just the journalists, or both, people responded favorably to his criticism of the media.[34]

Not surprisingly, the Texas tycoon became an integral part of the new-media equation in the minds of reporters. Qualitatively, journalists almost automatically equated his candidacy with the new media. At least they did in 1992. According to journalists, Perot: "legitimized the talk shows as campaign vehicles" (Larry King); "was determined to circumvent the Old Media by running a Wizard of Oz campaign that existed almost entirely behind the curtain of television" (Howard Kurtz); "had exposed the press's failings and its strengths" (Tom Rosenstiel); "seems to have thought he could schmooze his way to the White House without engag-ing any of the mediating institutions of American politics, especially the news media" (Tom Morganthau); was "the ultimate talk-show guest" (Joe Klein); "largely ignored reporters" (Gail Pennington); ran a cam-paign like "a postmodern undertaking that so far exists almost entirely on the airwaves and in the columns of newspapers and newsmagazines" (Howard Kurtz); "has one tool every target of the media would welcome, almost limitless resources to take himself and his beliefs directly to the public, unedited, unfiltered, unprocessed by us" (Jeff Greenfield); was "the TV candidate" (Marvin Kalb, Barry Golson, Peter Ross Range); and made Larry King "a household name because of . . . [his] frequent appearances on his interview show. Perot also proved that millions would tune in to TV lectures about such topics as the economy" (*Louisville Courier-Journal*).[35]

Whether Perot was the catalyst for this type of campaigning, an accidental beneficiary of it, or just its handy symbol, his impact seemed boundless in 1992—both politically and journalistically. He had helped respark public interest in politics and journalists' interest in the public. Even when critics said they personally distrusted Perot, most agreed that the combination of an active electorate and a responsive media had made for a livelier, more satisfying political year. Ross Perot did one thing more in 1992. He inspired the man who would go on to win the presidency and who would do so from the oddest of springboards.

Sax and Talk in the Month of June

Though the talk show campaign was underway during the primaries, it had not prominently established itself until June. Perot's definite commitment to the contest that month was one reason. The other was a rather unusual appearance by Bill Clinton on *Arsenio Hall*, a Fox Network program characterized by a low-key format and something other than a Wonder bread audience. The Clinton team did not have a great deal to lose at this point. Negative news coverage of Clinton had reached its height, and the campaign seemed headed for disaster. Staffers wre frantically trying to stall reporters like Jeff Gerth of the *New York Times*, who were only then just learning about the governor's involvement in a failed real estate venture known as Whitewater.[36] *The New Republic* magazine felt confident enough to predict the outcome of the race by headlining "Why Clinton Can't Win" on its May 4, 1992 cover. Clinton, his media consultant, Mandy Grunwald, and other key aides decided that voters were learning too little about the "real" Bill Clinton, so in a strategy dubbed "The Manhattan Project," Clinton would henceforth use direct-access media as much as possible and the mainstream press as sparingly as possible or only as necessary.[37] The Fox late-night program offered one such opportunity.

Talk show host Arsenio Hall was, as usual, all giggles for his program on June 3, 1992. On this night, though, the squirming schoolboy routine seemed a little more natural. Governor and presidential candidate Bill Clinton, accoutered in zoot suit and sunglasses, was playing saxophone with the band during the show's opening and soloed "Heartbreak Hotel" before a typically animated crowd. Before beginning his monologue, Hall quieted the audience, thanked Clinton for the music, then kidded him: "Okay, just ignore me right now 'cause this is the part of my show that politicians hate." Then, after a few seconds, he added, "Of course, I'll talk about the other guys." It was all part of the chatty mirth show business is famous for, which did not fail to attract the notice of wary journalists.

In an editorial for the *Washington Post*, William Raspberry worried that despite the perception that reporters ought to cover "the issues" during the campaign, they were inevitably forced to write about less important matters. "Would you like yours to be the only newspaper whose reporter neglected . . . the gaffes and gossip? Would you like yours to be the only network to feature 'white papers' while your competitors were going with sex, sin and saxophone playing?"[38] Journalists, he said, inevitably wind up dwelling on racehorse (who's ahead, how far) and electability news,[39] which regrettably meant covering Bill Clinton's appearance on *Arsenio Hall*, for example. In other words, Raspberry appears not to assign much journalistic importance to Clinton's appearance on the program. But he seems to change his mind near the end of his column, because after talking about the need for more "serious" information from candidates about "fiscal restraint" and "balanced budgets," he suddenly reconsiders his priorities, conceding that perhaps we do just want to know the basics about political candidates:

What is this guy really like? What worries him, excites or amuses him, impels him to seek the presidency? And there's no one to tell us these things. What candidate in his right mind would tell a reporter that he's not sure if the deficit can be reduced significantly in the near term, or that most classical music bores him or that he's always had this 'thing' about being president? That sort of candor would be deadly, which is why we get staff-approved sound bites. Maybe what we want (and don't dare admit) is a suspension of adversarial journalism in favor of a series of friendly conversations with the candidates.[40]

Raspberry goes on to challenge the assumption that tough, prosecutorial journalism is the only way to discover a candidate's real character or voice. Or, in other words, cattle-prodding a politician might not be the most efficient means to try to understand his views. As Larry King once said, "You don't have to jump across the desk to challenge [a candidate]."[41] "I never want to embarrass anyone. My role is to learn."[42]

Raspberry was right. And intellectual or political vacuity does not at any rate accurately describe the Clinton-Hall encounter. More went on than high-fives and small jokes.[43] After the first several minutes of the program, the two men settled into a discussion of racism and democracy, focusing on the then recent Los Angeles riots and what political leadership might do to resolve the scars evident there and elsewhere. Clinton insisted on the importance of "reconnecting people with the American community," and "reestablishing contact between people." Part of what he was talking about certainly involved "economic empowerment," but it also entailed a social and political facet. The riots, Clinton suggested, were the ugly side of a kind of activism that did produce results. "Those folks are invisible until they raise hell." What both local and national leaders had to do was provide (free of charge) or encourage the use of resources with which residents could create positive, sustaining forms of community engagement. Positions like these were certainly somewhat vague but appeared sincere (as conversations between people do often tend toward frankness) and did have the merit of being more coherent than the same sentiment expressed in a seven-second sound bite.

Many journalists did not remember the program that way, however. They only saw the joking and the saxophone playing and thought, "This is not how a presidential candidate is supposed to act." "Am I such an old fogey that I thought that it was undignified?" Barbara Walters asked on ABC's *This Week with David Brinkley*. "I mean, there is something about the presidential candidate with his shades on, playing the saxophone that's endearing on the one hand, but not very dignified."[44] Syndicated *New York Times* columnist Tom Wicker seconded her suspicion:

I don't think a president has to maintain a certain stuffed-shirt dignity or a presidential candidate, but I don't know—the association with jazz music and dark shades and *The Arsenio Hall Show*, I don't think that's an asset in running for the presidency. And I don't mean to knock Arsenio Hall at all, but I mean, I think people associate that with a different kind of notoriety. [F]or a guy to appear on television, playing jazz, with dark shades on *The Arsenio Hall Show* after midnight, I don't think that enhances his standing on family values.[45]

Perhaps Bush press secretary Torie Clarke had inspired these sentiments. The day after Clinton's meeting with Arsenio Hall, Clarke lambasted both the candidate's performance and his judgment: "I thought it was embarrassing. . . . He looked like a sad John Belushi wannabe. . . . I don't think most Americans want to see their president wearing a goofy tie and sunglasses and blowing on a saxophone, and then talking about smoking pot with a late-night TV host."[46]

"Bullshit," replied Mandy Grunwald, who had promoted the *Arsenio* appearance. "This is how people get information."[47] She had outlined her talk show strategy to Clinton in April and explained that its benefit was to showcase his personal side, "to convey biography and personality," she recalled later to none other than Larry King. "You can't do that on the evening news."[48] Grunwald believed the "undignified" label talk shows earned for conducting programs with political candidates was unfair and untrue. "We were trying to explain that this was a person, not a caricature like the cartoons in your newspaper but a person who has a life . . . I think explaining who you are is not unpresidential." In a few months, President Bush was able to do just that—explain who he was—in forums like *Larry King Live*, and at once he recognized the feeling of liberation they gave him. "The great thing about this," he told King in October, "is I don't have to have some guy come on the minute the debate's over or you and I finish a question: [feigns holding a microphone and mimics the sound of a self-important journalist] 'Well, it looks like Larry King won this round. Looks like Bill Clinton won the debate again.' Can't people decide without a filter?" Grunwald and Bush both expressed the candidates' thirst to reach voters.

Raspberry emphasized a corollary: citizens wanted to connect with candidates and hungered for an honest level of conversation missing in most encounters between politicians and journalists. Instead, voters were shuffled into the role of spectator and treated to fish swaps in which candidates traded cold, canned responses for the icy cynicism of journalists. No wonder mainstream media were turning people away. Journalists were hampering dialogue, not opening the way for it. And citizens were tired of the rigamarole that accompanied spectatorship anyway. "We don't even know how to talk to one another in a truly democratic way anymore," syndicated columnist Molly Ivins complained in the middle of the year. The lapse of political communication made civic activism less likely, she said, because it erodes people's faith in their ability to control events.[49] Some politicians and many more journalists could not see the growing public frustration, and so they failed to understand either the reason for voter apathy or the popularity and importance of alternative forums available to political candidates to contact those disaffected voters. Larry King put the matter succinctly: "The 'Arsenio' controversy was a classic example of dismissive Beltway dwellers laughing—even though the joke was really on them. . . . It was a smart move."[50] Even informal conversations, it seems, had their place in democratic politics, and they were in no way "inferior" to punditry expressed in print. "The written word, we sometimes forget, was invented as a crude if useful substitute for the real thing."[51]

Eventually, even the reluctant Bush campaign team came to appreciate this view, despite the fact that it had first branded the idea "weird," "wacky," and beneath the dignity of the White House. By the time the Republicans responded in kind, though, it was too late. "I think we virtually lost the election," Bush spokesman Marlin Fitzwater told Larry King in 1993, "before anybody realized the wisdom of doing these shows."[52] In August, even the conservative *National Review* was needling Bush to get with the times—often as it simultaneously spoofed the influence of the talk shows in numerous cartoons and poems.[53] Before the year's end, Bush capitulated and ultimately visited all three network morning programs more than once (and ABC's *Good Morning America* seven times), appeared on *Larry King Live* three times, and even showed up on MTV—four months after chiding Clinton for doing the same thing.[54] Perot appeared on twice as many such programs as Bush, and Clinton three times as many as Bush.[55] Yet Bush's reversal of campaign policy proved that the new media had eclipsed the old, and that if winning the election depended on courting the former, if it involved answering call-in questions from viewers on talk shows, candidates would predictably do so. "[W]e are game players," Clinton tactician James Carville observed. "We are not rule makers."[56]

Bush was the last candidate to get on the bandwagon, but some journalists never did. Again, at any rate, the reckoning for many first came in June, when Clinton's appearance on *Arsenio Hall* graphically marked the new manner of political campaigning. William Raspberry's questions mentioned above capture the powerful need journalists felt to make sense of the new media. Raspberry's case is a typical one too, for in general, June was the month when most of his colleagues initially grappled with the emerging talk show phenomenon. A Nexis search of coverage by three dozen newspapers of Ross Perot's visits to *Larry King Live* (there had been a second one in April) confirms this discovery, and a comparable search of coverage by news magazines and two individual newspapers mirrors this news pattern closely. The conformity of coverage among all these sources verifies that June occasioned the wake-up call for journalists to start paying attention to the talk shows and similar forums. It also testifies to the unforgettable visual impact of Bill Clinton's *Arsenio* appearance.

CONCLUSION

From the summer until the election, Bill Clinton set the standard for talk show performances. He was still a masterful political candidate in other respects: he was supremely well informed on most major domestic issues—a real policy wonk, everyone said; he was a productive fundraiser; and he was an almost inexhaustible campaigner, someone who never seemed to tire of shaking hands, meeting voters, making friends and contacts. But no one, not even Ross Perot, demonstrated the flair and ease with which he talked to television hosts, answered callers' questions, or engaged in give-and-take discussion with ordinary citizens. His soothing ability to calm and relate to and ingratiate himself with voters earned Clinton a reputation as the politician most in touch with the electorate. Indeed, "his entire candidacy reflected a willingness to appeal directly to the public."[57] For all his foibles, Americans perceived him as the candidate who best understood them, and that is why he won the presidency in 1992. The television talk show, in short, was the perfect medium for Bill Clinton.

Such forums, of course, were not really new. Politicians have always known that shaking a citizen's hand or kissing his six-month-old toddler is inherently more effective than delivering complicated stump speeches. Many candidates and journalists had apparently forgotten that axiom, the latter perhaps because it was in their interest to do so, to promote their own role as necessary mediators. The personnel associated with unconventional formats, by contrast, didn't much care; they were happy just to have booked a hot "talent" or famous celebrity to lift their ratings and boost their market share. The new media were therefore ready and available to serve politicians. Clinton was the first spectacular beneficiary of the new system, elected to the presidency because many people believed that he appreciated their problems, cared about fixing those things, and knew how to do it.[58] But within a half-dozen years he would find his prestige challenged by those same media, as well as others. Indeed, his political success in the 1990s prepared the stage for a whole new era in which the most cutting-edge communications technology in existence was inextricably mixed with politics, and by the end of the decade Clinton would find his reputation probed, skewered, and roasted on each of the new media.

NOTES

1. Thomas Friedman, "The Inauguration," *New York Times* (January 21, 1993), p. A1.

2. Walter Goodman, "Critic's Notebook: In the Inaugural of Inclusion, All the Arts Are In," *New York Times* (January 21, 1993), p. C20.

3. Quoted in Maureen Dowd and Frank Rich, "The Inauguration: The Boomers' Ball," *New York Times* (January 21, 1993), p. A11.

4. James Fallows, " 'Their' War, 'Our' Guilt," *Washington Post* (February 16, 1992), p. C1.

5. Dan Balz, "Clinton, Kerry: A New Set of Questions," *Washington Post* (January 18, 1992), p. A1.

6. Clinton is obviously not the only prominent politician to tell fish stories about his record during the Vietnam War. Dan Quayle's fib that his stint in the Indiana National Guard had been only a "kind of way-station en route to Vietnam" rang hollow to those old enough to remember. "Any man of Quayle's generation has no doubt whatsoever about why one joined the Guard in those days." James Fallows, " 'Their' War, 'Our' Guilt," *Washington Post*.

7. Alan M. Dershowitz, *Sexual McCarthyism: Clinton, Starr, and the Emerging Constitutional Crisis* (New York: Basic Books, 1998), p. 146.

8. Quoted by Roger Simon, "And the Campaign Isn't Even Tough Yet," *Los Angeles Times* (April 5, 1992), p. E7.

9. Ibid.

10. David Von Drehle, "Bill Clinton's Movers and Shapers," *Washington Post* (March 23, 1992), p. D1.

11. "Star-Crossed Lovers," *Time* (August 17, 1992), p. 33.

12. George Stephanopoulos, *All Too Human: A Political Education* (Boston: Little, Brown, 1999), p. 90.

13. Quoted by Karen Ball, "Clinton's Media Whiz: Mandy Grunwald," Associated Press Wire (September 28, 1992).

14. Paul Begala, quoted in "The Clinton Years," ABC, *Nightline* (January 8, 2001).

15. Steve Weinstein, "The Courtship of the MTV Voter," *Los Angeles Times* (June 18, 1992), p. F1.

16. Mack Reed, "Clinton Talks to Local Voters Via Satellite," *Los Angeles Times* (June 25, 1992), p. B1.

17. Edwin Yoder, "Despite Southern Roots, Bill Clinton Is No Carter," *Atlanta Journal and Constitution* (May 5, 1992), p. A29.

18. Shari Roan, "All the Presidents' Miens," *Los Angeles Times* (August 12, 1996), p. E1.

19. Ibid.

20. David Maraniss, *First in His Class: A Biography of Bill Clinton* (New York: Simon & Schuster, 1995), p. 408. See also Dick Morris, *Behind the Oval*

Office: Winning the Presidency in the Nineties (New York: Random House, 1997), p. 99.

21. This assertion is based on an analysis of *Readers' Guide to Periodical Literature*, 1992.

22. *USA Today* (February 19, 1992), p. D3.

23. *TV Guide* (May 9, 1992), p. 9.

24. *Atlanta Journal and Constitution* (November 1, 1992), p. N1.

25. *Rolling Stone* (December 10–24, 1992), p. 196.

26. Perot continued: "So, as Lech Walesa said, 'Words are plentiful, but deeds are precious.' And this is my way of saying, 'Will you get in the ring? Will you put the gloves on? And do you care enough about this country to stay the course?' " (*Larry King Live*, CNN, February 20, 1992).

27. Larry King, with Mark Stencel, *On the Line: The New Road to the White House* (New York: Harcourt Brace & Company, 1993), p. 28.

28. Ibid.

29. Martha FitzSimon, ed., *The Finish Line: Covering the Campaign's Final Days* (New York: Freedom Forum Media Studies Center, 1993), p. 124.

30. *This Week with David Brinkley*, ABC, June 7, 1992.

31. Martha FitzSimon, ed., *Covering the Presidential Primaries* (New York: Freedom Forum Media Studies Center, 1992), p. 28.

32. Howard Kurtz, "Media Circus," *Washington Post Magazine* (July 12, 1992), p.W19. Ben Bagdikian pushes the criticism further by indicting the whole practice of journalism during all of the 1980s. Bagdikian, "Journalism of Joy," *Mother Jones* (May/June 1992).

33. Richard Berke, "Sound Bites Grow at CBS," *New York Times* (July 11, 1992), p. 7.

34. The other candidates were quick to join in the old-media-bashing chorus. According to press ombudsman Richard Harwood, virtually everyone in the race, including Clinton, Tom Harkin, and Jerry Brown, were equally quick to engage in "Grade B demagoguery." Harwood, "What Conspiracy?" *Washington Post* (March 1, 1992), p. C6.

35. Larry King, *On the Line*, p. 28; Howard Kurtz, *Media Circus: The Trouble with America's Newspapers* (New York: Random House, 1993), p. 287; Tom Rosenstiel, *Strange Bedfellows: How Television and the Presidential Candidates Changed American Politics, 1992* (New York: Hyperion, 1993), p. 196; Tom Morgenthau, "The Quitter: Why Perot Bowed Out," *Newsweek* (July 27, 1992), p. 28; Joe Klein, "The Bill Clinton Show," *Newsweek* (October 26, 1992), p. 35; Gail Pennington, *St. Louis Post-Dispatch* (July 7, 1992), p. D13; Howard Kurtz, *Washington Post* (May 23, 1992), p. A4; Jeff Greenfield, ABC, *World News Tonight* (May 29, 1992); Marvin Kalb, CNN, *Reliable Sources* (October 24, 1992); Barry Golson and Peter Ross Range, *TV Guide* (June 20, 1992), p. 5; *Louisville Courier-Journal* (May 30, 1993), p. T3.

36. James B. Stewart, *Blood Sport: The President and His Adversaries* (New York: Simon & Schuster, 1996), p. 192.

37. Larry King, *On the Line*, pp. 31–37.

38. *Washington Post* (June 10, 1992), p. A23.

39. "[D]ammit, it *is* a horse race. We didn't create it," ABC News political director Hal Bruno remarked in the spring (Quoted in *Covering the Presidential Primaries*, Freedom Forum Media Studies Center, June 1992, p. 29).

40. Ibid.

41. "The New Media in the 1992 Campaign," Harvard University Joan Shorenstein Barone Center roundtable, C-SPAN, Oct. 2, 1992.

42. Larry King, interviewed by Arthur Unger, "Larry King: 'Everyman with a Mike,' " *Television Quarterly*, vol. 26, no. 3, 1993, p. 35.

43. Those certainly occurred, though. When pressed, Clinton admitted favoring the younger-Elvis postage stamp.

44. *This Week with David Brinkley*, ABC, June 7, 1992.

45. Ibid.

46. *Washington Post* (June 5, 1992), p. C2.

47. Quoted in Tom Rosenstiel, *Strange Bedfellows: How Television and the Presidential Candidates Changed American Politics, 1992* (New York: Hyperion Press, 1993), pp. 174–75; see also Larry King, *On the Line*, p. 37.

48. Larry King, *On the Line*, pp. 32, 37.

49. Molly Ivins, "Read My Lipstick," *Mother Jones*, May/June 1992, p. 13. Barbara Ehrenreich repeats this argument in her article, "Who's on Main Street?" (*Mother Jones*, July/August 1992, pp. 40–46, 75): "The whole notion of government—above the level of school boards and zoning ordinances—has become hypothetical, difficult for the average citizen to verify with his or her sensory equipment. Oh, we know it's there, but the evidence increasingly comes from our television sets: the gulf war; the State of the Union address (with a buildup almost matching the war's); and *Crossfire* every night after dinner. It is government-as-spectacle."

50. Larry King, *On the Line*, p. 37.

51. Richard Wright, "Channeling," *The New Republic* (June 15, 1992), p. 46.

52. Ibid., p. 39.

53. See, for example, W. H. Von Dreele, "For Mr. Bush's Handlers," *National Review* (August 3, 1992), p. 22.

54. Martha FitzSimon, ed., *The Finish Line: Covering the Campaign's Final Days* (New York: Freedom Forum Media Studies Center, January 1993), pp. 124–125.

55. Ibid.

56. *This Week with David Brinkley*, ABC, June 14, 1992.

57. Dale A. Herbeck, "Presidential Debate as Political Ritual: Clinton vs Bush vs Perot," in *Bill Clinton on Stump, State, and Stage: The Rhetorical Road*

to the White House, ed. Stephen A. Smith (Fayetteville: University of Arkansas Press, 1994), p. 268.

58. Even when Bush led in the polls in the spring of 1992, his most important liability, as perceived by voters, was his inability to do just that, while empathy was widely touted by most supporters of Clinton as his most important asset. For early interpretation of these polls, see David Broder and Richard Morin, "For Swing Voters, Not Much Choice: Critical Election Bloc Flunks Bush on Empathy, Clinton on Integrity," *Washington Post* (March 20, 1992), p. A1.

2

First-Term Follies

INTRODUCTION

George Stephanopoulos's first press conference was a disaster. His boss, Bill Clinton, was under fire for the nomination of Zoe Baird for attorney general, a woman who hadn't paid taxes for her nanny. The president was also getting grilled by conservatives for his promise to end the ban on gays in the military, then by liberals for appearing to back away from that pledge. Worst of all, though, reporters were furious that the passageway between the press room in the White House and the press secretary's office had been recently sealed off. "I want to tell you," veteran wire-service correspondent Helen Thomas lectured Stephanopoulos, "I've been here since Kennedy, and those steps have never been blocked to us, and the press secretary's office has never been off limits. Ever."[1]

Stephanopoulos made excuses, but knew they were right. In his memoir, *All Too Human*, he admittted that he was unprepared for the appearance. He had not come with facts, or even colorful personal information about the Clintons to give to the reporters gathered to hear him. He had not brought another speaker to field questions on such matters as foreign policy; he wanted the limelight all to himself. And he began sweating profusely. "Welcome to the big leagues," Thomas told him at the end of the thirty-minute encounter. The first official press conference hosted by Clinton's first communications director epitomized overall White House public relations during most of the president's first term: hasty, unprofessional, and ineffective.

Yet, Bill Clinton was a savvy student of the presidency. As many observers have pointed out, he adapted quickly while on the job, making mistakes but recovering from them, learning, and improving along the way. He made administrative changes, hired new people, and grew into the role. Two of the personnel decisions Clinton had to wrestle slowly with were the positions of communications director and press secretary. The whole area of press relations, in fact, had to be examined anew— as it does by every new administration striving to keep up with professional and technological changes. But the establishment of an effective public relations operation also hinges critically on the personal relationship between the president and his crew of communications specialists. Whatever their credentials and capabilities, in other words, those persons serving as liaisons to the public and the press must understand the president well, and know the limits of their own relationship with him, to work efficiently.

The evolution of that process seemed to transpire rather slowly during the Clinton administration, the first term in particular. By 1997, things had become almost smooth. Then came a crisis for which all the good PR in the world would have mattered little: the Lewinsky scandal and subsequent impeachment proceedings. At that point, the president's staff was simply fighting for survival. That episode will be discussed in a separate chapter. For now, I will look more carefully at the early Clinton years, as well as a quieter, more routine side of White House communications. These pages will address such subjects as Clinton's press secretaries, press conferences, and overall press relations. What they amount to, I believe, is a record of awkward beginnings and only gradually improving performance, what I call the administration's "first-term follies."

1993: CHAOS

White House spokesman George Stephanopoulos admitted years later that he had gone into that first official press conference woefully unprepared. He had failed to anticipate the degree to which the press might dwell exhaustively on a single subject or try his patience with innumerable variations of the same basic question. He may also have gone in overly confident. Perhaps, too, he and his fellow staffers, many of them not much older or experienced than he, were the unfortunate beneficiaries of unrealistically high expectations. Journalist Christopher Hanson noted some of the accolades Stephanopoulos received at the end of the 1992 campaign, and compared them with the press's reconsideration six months later. *U.S. News and World Report*, for example, dubbed the Clinton adviser "boy wonder" in December, "former boy wonder" in June. Likewise, *Time*'s Margaret Carlson proclaimed Stephanopoulos "one of the savviest communicators in the business" in November, but an utter failure by the summer. "Anything's better than George," she wrote.[2] Other journalists were coming to the same disappointing conclusion. *New York Times* reporter Thomas Friedman complained that despite good policy decisions, "something is missing in that White House because it's not delivering on the other end. It was truly depressing. You say to yourself, 'We're at a watershed moment in this country's history and these people are so muffing it!' Yesterday I just wanted to get a hook and pull George Stephanopoulos off stage and say, 'George, go back, get your ducks in order, and then come out here, because this is too serious.' "[3]

As Stephanopoulos himself came to understand, the entire White House was operating inefficiently in 1993. Meetings were called haphazardly and attended by too many people, including junior staffers still disposed toward college-style bull sessions. Valuable time was wasted on irrelevant subjects. "We were blind to the importance of structure," Stephanopoulos recalled. "We didn't have enough respect . . . for the office."[4] The disorganization showed in "rancorous press briefings" and in Stephanopoulos's "abrasive and secretive style."[5] Stephanopoulos did not last long. On Memorial Day weekend, President Clinton juggled his staff to make room for someone who did fully appreciate the demands of the Oval Office: David Gergen, a journalist and former adviser to Presidents Nixon, Ford, and Reagan. Gergen was given the title of counselor, while Mark Gearan was made new communications director. Stephanopoulos, a kind of fallen Icarus, became "senior adviser."[6]

Clinton decided, however, to retain the services of Dee Dee Myers, his first press secretary. The first woman to hold the job, the thirty-one-year-old Myers was also the youngest press secretary in American history. Myers's youth—and, she insists, her gender—caused her problems from the beginning. For six months, Stephanopoulos had conducted the daily briefings himself. Though she'd won the position, "she didn't get the salary, nor the big office, nor the access to the president that customarily go with that job."[7] As a result, she often operated in the dark, and with dire consequences. In June 1994, for example, the president failed to inform her about an American air strike against Iraq, so she wound up giving journalists false information—"an enormous black mark for a press secretary."[8] "On . . . good days," a *USA Today* writer recalled, she was the "image of spunky, youthful energy with just the right shade of California cool"; on "bad days, she was the symbol—often through no fault of her own—of an overwhelmed and inexperienced staff."[9] Myers was kept out of the inner circle, out of the "white boys' club," as she called it. Journalists liked Myers personally and sympathized with her predicament, but ultimately could not trust what she said because she was "continually plagued by the perception of being outside the loop when key decisions were made."[10]

Meanwhile, the president remained vulnerable on other fronts. Mishaps, some of them spectacular, occurred a little too regularly. A teleprompter operator once fed the wrong speech into the computer for a televised address. Clinton remained cool and ad-libbed beautifully, while an alerted Stephanopoulos scrambled for the correct computer disk. But afterward, the president screamed at aides for the unjustifiable screwup. Less conspicuous episodes, such as the frantic, last-minute editing of a State of the Union address in a car on its way to the Capitol, were even more worrisome, though, because of the risk and sloppiness they demonstrated. When told of the way televised speeches were hastily composed and prepared in the White House, former Bush aide Tony Snow told Stephanopoulos, "George, you guys are bungee jumping without a rope."[11]

Overall, the president's oratory left much to be desired. He had entered office with a well-earned reputation for spellbinding stumping and tireless talk. But campaigning is not the same thing as governing. Nor is the effective rhetoric of a candidate like that of an incumbent. Each requires different tones, body language, and degrees of formality, and it took several years for Clinton to master the distinctions.[12] While Bill Clinton had always demonstrated a knack for informal speaking—for ad-libbing, conversation, and one-on-one mingling—delivering stately speeches was still new terrain for him. His extremely brief inaugural address, for example, failed "to rally the American public around a clear vision of their national mission."[13] So soon after his campaign, the president was probably still in election mode.

In less structured settings, the president was more successful. Even so, Clinton waited two months before giving his first full-fledged press conference—March 23. Thereafter he followed the lead of his predecessor, George Bush, and appeared at about two a month. Both men met the press on a more frequent basis than did other presidents of the twentieth century.[14] Though Clinton would go "into bunker mode at scandal time," he could not quite afford politically to lie low, so instead he tried to maintain the image of accessibility and public confidence. Then, too, in a changed media environment, average Americans don't distinguish between formal press conferences and ordinary news footage of presidential appearances. As former Republican press secretary Marlin Fitzwater explained it, "I don't think you could find five people in America who think President Clinton hasn't been on television enough or hasn't been holding press conferences. They see him every night. They see him answering questions. So you ask anybody in Iowa, 'Does Bill Clinton not give press conferences?' They'd say, 'You're crazy. I see him all the time.' "[15] Fitzwater also pointed out, with admitted envy, the Clinton public relations team's tactic of always having an aide or other spokesperson on talk shows to get the administration's view across.

The White House also introduced a new forum in presidential communications: the televisual town hall meeting. As a political candidate, Clinton had excelled in this venue, delivering star performances at unstructured campaign rallies, at question-and-answer appearances such as his MTV and *Larry King Live* visits, and, most famously, at the second presidential debate in Richmond, Virginia, October 15, when he stole the show. In the burgeoning culture of *Oprah* and *Donahue*, Bill Clinton showed a flair for captivating small audiences before live television. But even more than the average talk show host, Clinton thrived on the give-and-take dynamic provided by audience participation. The former law school professor loved to turn the tables on people gathered to hear him talk by putting them on the spot and asking them questions. In 1992, after receiving rave reviews for his participation in town hall-style meetings, he promised that, as president, he would continue the practice.

And during his first two years in the White House he did. Within a six-month period the president hosted two such meetings, one in Michigan in September, the other in North Carolina in April. Both tackled the thorny issue of health care reform. Yet neither proved the success Clinton had hoped for. While the mechanics of each performance went well enough, the president nevertheless conveyed the image of an anxious politician desperate to win support. The appearances seemed, well, unpresidential. As students of political communication have explained, such a format is more ideally suited to campaigning than to governing, because it overexposes White House leadership and antagonizes the Washington press corps, which is unaccustomed to watching from the sidelines.[16] "The modern presidency," Howard Kurtz has written, is "above all, a media presidency."[17] But not just any media will do. As President Clinton learned the hard way in 1993 and 1994, too much talk can handicap a political leader as much as too little.

Overall, Clinton's first year in office had gone badly. The tragedy in Waco, Texas, where a two-month siege ended in April with the deaths of eighty members of a commune as well as four federal agents, managed to make the administration look both thuggish and inept. The White House's "don't ask—don't tell" compromise in July had pleased no one but infuriated everybody in the controversy over allowing gays in the military. Health care reform seemed to be stumbling along haphazardly. And even the Democratic Congress could not see eye-to-eye with the president on the budget. According to White House budget manager Leon Panetta, there arose a widespread fear that the administration had become a prisoner to "chaos." With the summer suicide of Clinton's longtime friend and deputy White House counsel Vince Foster, the chaos seemed permeated with grief and despair.

Worse, the mysterious circumstances surrounding Foster's death fanned rumor and speculation, which the president did nothing to abate with his stubborn silence. Mishandling of some of the documents in Foster's possession eventually fueled a whole cottage industry of conspiracy theories and further heightened journalists' suspicions of the White House. Reporters began going on the offensive and became more aggressive—a surprising development when you consider that twice as many of their ranks had gone to work for Clinton in his first two years than for Bush in all four of his.[18] "To the extent the Clinton administration ever enjoyed a honeymoon," *Wall Street Journal* reporter James Stewart noted, "it ended on July 20, 1993."[19] Desperate, the Clintons brought in Stewart to keep the lines of communication open between the White House and the press, but gradually those lines were closed off as the first couple soon retreated instinctively into their private world. In the end, Stewart concluded, they "proved no different than their predecessors, deeply enmeshed in a Washington culture so inured to partisan distortion and spin that truth is the most frightening prospect of all."[20]

1994: HUBRIS

Five days after his inauguration in 1993, Bill Clinton had chosen his wife, Hillary, to spearhead a task force on health care reform. Throughout that year and the next, the first lady presided over unwieldy discussions that showed neither the freedom of a think tank seminar nor the discipline of a congressional committee session. The White House failed to bring together political alliances capable of supporting specific legislation. Instead, special interests drifted away quickly and hardened into adamantine opposition—drug companies, for example, shelling out millions of dollars in advertising to squelch the Clinton proposals. Equally damaging, perhaps, was the president's commando-style rhetoric, in which he routinely brandished the word "crisis." That language frightened Americans, who were dissatisfied with the state of health care in the country but obviously even leerier of drastic changes. Indeed, "Clinton's 'crisis' rhetoric made the whole situation worse in the end. . . . A declaration of crisis . . . usually polarizes rhetoric between the 'threat' and the 'threatened.' "[21] In August, surveys showed that a majority of Americans disapproved of the Clintons' plan, believing, however correctly, that they had "more to lose than gain" from proposed reform.[22] Once again, the president's oratory had failed him. And in September, the Democrats abandoned the effort, a quiet defeat that damaged the administration's credibility.

Though his State of the Union address earlier in 1994 did bring him the traditional bounce in ratings, which such speeches normally do, the public's blessing quickly dissipated. The same month, the conservative *American Spectator* published a notorious cover story by David Brock about Bill Clinton's adulterous affairs in Arkansas and the troopers he allegedly recruited to assist him. The article, entitled "His Cheatin' Heart," was not supposed to disclose the names of the women involved with Clinton, but, because of a copyeditor's mistake, a single reference to "Paula" was left undeleted. That small omission would have large consequences. On May 4, Paula Jones filed a sexual harassment lawsuit against the president, and his popularity sank even further as Americans, rightly or wrongly, sympathetically or not, came to view him as a "tabloid" celebrity. After Jones filed her lawsuit, the president's attorney, Bob Bennett, held a press conference to denounce the litigation and did so in striking language: "This complaint is tabloid trash with a legal caption on it. . . . This suit is about publicity, it's about talk shows, it's about money."[23] It was certainly not a seemly association for the President of the United States.

In the meantime, the continuing investigation into the president's Whitewater investment venture was bleeding the White House like an open wound. Reporters were descending in waves on small Arkansas towns then to look into this obscure real estate deal and its connections

to a shoddily run savings-and-loan institution managed by Clinton pal
Jim McDougal. For months the president had been ignoring requests by
the *Washington Post* and the *New York Times* that the administration
release documents relevant to those events, including the Clintons' com-
plete tax returns. Presidential advisers David Gergen and George Stephanopoulos had argued fiercely throughout 1993 for cooperating with
the press and laying their cards on the table, but the views of Hillary
Clinton and Bernard Nussbaum prevailed instead.[24] By January 1994,
however, the pressure was unbearable. With even some Democrats demanding an inquiry, President Clinton reluctantly ordered Attorney General Janet Reno to appoint an independent counsel. In retrospect, then,
the stonewalling seems to have been not just futile but counterproductive.
Journalist James Stewart admitted being baffled: "[N]othing in the Clintons' past, on its face, seems to explain the pattern of evasion, half-
truths, and misstatements. . . . [Their] drop-by-drop concessions gave
credence to their critics and undermined their integrity."[25]

After six months' work, Independent Counsel Robert Fiske found no
evidence of wrongdoing, but a three-judge panel named a new counsel,
Kenneth Starr, and House and Senate banking committees started their
own investigations into the matter. Hardly a day went by without some
mention in the news about the investigations. And, finally, amid congressional gridlock in the fall, much of the public grew impatient and
irritable. The president's approval numbers fell sharply throughout the
whole of 1994, and in November they reached historic depths with the
congressional midterm election. Two pollsters concluded that "[b]etween
his inauguration and his two-year rating . . . Clinton suffered some of the
lowest ratings of any president during a similar period."[26]

The mid-term election results reflected the administration's dismal
standing in the polls. However much predicted at the time, though, November's congressional election was devastating for the president and
his party. For the first time in two generations, Republicans gained control of both houses of Congress. The political movement that became
known as the Republican Revolution hit the president hard and clinched
his decision, one especially urged by his wife and his new chief of staff,
Leon Panetta, to shake up the staff once more. Up for review were Media
Adviser Mandy Grunwald, pollster Stan Greenberg, and Press Secretary
Dee Dee Myers—none of whom any longer enjoyed Clinton's confidence.[27] Besides, the president was both furious about and frustrated with
the outcome of the elections. As his image, and that of his administration,
were in crisis, he struggled to find the source of his woes.

In an end-of-the-year interview with media critic Ken Auletta, former White House counsel Lloyd Cutler expressed dissatisfaction with Clinton's relationship to the press up to that point. Clinton, Cutler said, "makes a bigger effort with the press" than President Carter had, but apparently was no more successful at dealing with journalists than his Democratic predecessor. "He's just gotten angry at the press," Cutler explained.[28] In any case, the first half of Clinton's first term was a particularly bad one, and the president's poor media relations were part of the reason. Of the half-dozen presidents she had covered in her career as a broadcast journalist, ABC News's Ann Compton believed that Clinton stood out as the only one who had done "everything in his power to go around, under, and away from the White House press corps."[29] Bill Clinton simply did not trust journalists, and he tended to take personally public criticism about him. Periods of scandal only made him all the more reclusive and bitter. "It has been an acrimonious two years," Carl Cannon and Nelson Schwartz of the *Baltimore Sun* concluded, "what with Whitewater, filibustering Republicans, Paula C. Jones and the often dueling arrogance of the Clintonites and the press corps."[30] Cannon and Schwartz wrote that since Clinton was "highly suspicious" of journalists, he accordingly gave short shrift to his press secretaries, and therefore this uncooperative attitude had spread throughout the administration.

Dee Dee Myers was *the* case in point. She had not yet done well in her job as press secretary. Then again, she had not been allowed to do well. "Outside the inner circle, faced with a dizzying array of issues, handed misinformation and disinformation by higher-ups, Myers foundered," a *Washington Post* correspondent wrote.[31] In October, she did an end-run around Leon Panetta, who was poised to fire her, by going straight to President Clinton. She emerged from that meeting with her job, a raise, and additional privileges. But she had only bought herself a few months' time.[32] She had still not won the president's confidence, and she continued to struggle to keep well informed about day-to-day changes in policy goals and in emphases in publicity. The Clintons finally persuaded her to leave, and she dutifully resigned on December 23 after an emotional meeting with the president in the Oval Office. She did not exactly go quietly—and some in the press accused her of whimpering about her departure[33]—but a fuller account of what happened in those first years would have to wait until Jeffrey Birnbaum's 1996 book, *Madhouse*. All that Myers would say in 1994 was that it had been tough being a woman in the White House, but that she was grateful for the opportunity.

1995: STASIS

White House chief of staff Leon Panetta hired a seasoned political aide to replace Myers. Mike McCurry, at forty, had worked for a slew of Democratic governors and senators, before joining the State Department as a spokesperson with a distinguished reputation for levity. McCurry took over for Myers in January 1995 and hit a home run in his first at-bat with humorous references to his likely celibacy while a busy press secretary, and to his past association with unsuccessful Democratic politicians: "I've worked for a very long list of losers in my lifetime. Thanks for reminding me."[34] Reporters took to him immediately. McCurry announced his goal of improving relations between the press and the president, relations that had chilled so much by then that Clinton already seemed to dislike the correspondents as much as many of them disliked him. In four years of service, McCurry tried to treat them fairly while serving the president faithfully, and often he was forced to tilt noticeably toward the latter. A partisan streak, in fact, was sometimes mentioned as one of his shortcomings, even though not altogether one of his own making. Former ABC News correspondent Brit Hume explained: "He's a good press secretary because he knows the issues, he knows the politics and he knows how to talk to reporters. . . . But it's better to talk to him away from the daily briefing. It's clear that the White House had decided the briefings should be an aggressive exercise in salesmanship and argument—and McCurry is conducting it accordingly."[35]

Yet, McCurry never gave up his sense of humor or his low-key congeniality. Asked whether he would ever lie to the press, he quipped, "No, but I'd tell the truth slowly."[36] An "impish wit" and a fondness for reporters made him a hit with journalists. United Press International (UPI) correspondent Helen Thomas, for one, gave him a rave review: "He's created an atmosphere of friendliness—after we were spat upon and treated as the enemy. . . . They hired kids in this administration. They called us 'the Beast.' He changed it all. He created an atmosphere of civility."[37] Before long, most of the rest of the Washington press corps also accorded him genuine respect and affection. Some even compared McCurry to the legendary Jim Hagerty, press secretary under President Eisenhower.[38] Journalists valued Clinton's new spokesman for his personality, his honesty, and his knowledge. Perhaps most significantly they could identify with him as a peer. "No one in the history of the job did more to create a cozy salon atmosphere among reporters in the White House press room than . . . Mike McCurry," wrote one editor.[39] "They like McCurry and find him unfailingly good-humored," writer Godfrey Sperling reflected. "Most of all, they appreciate having a press secretary who is a part of Clinton's inner circle and who therefore is positioned to know from moment to moment what the president is thinking and intending to do."[40] CBS News correspondent Rita Braver agreed: "I think that he came in with three things that made a huge difference: access, authority and autonomy."[41]

Reporters also gave McCurry high marks for obtaining firsthand information for them, for bringing administration experts into press conferences, where they delivered attributable, on-the-record statements and helpful background information. "We never took the posture," McCurry later explained, that "the secretary of state or the president would be diminished if the staff people or the aides came out and briefed."[42] McCurry also pleased broadcasters by gradually extending the amount of camera time during the afternoon briefing. He did it, he said, because when the TV crews switched off their equipment, he found himself letting up: "I kind of relaxed and didn't keep my sharp edge and . . . focus."[43] Eventually, he allowed cameramen to shoot the entire briefing, a practice he came to regret only during the Lewinsky scandal.

Surprisingly, it was not always the scandals that made press relations most difficult for McCurry, but unexpected stories like the Oklahoma City bombing on April 19, 1995, when 169 people were killed. The magnitude of the tragedy fueled a ferocious media frenzy that bore down on McCurry with wild allegations about Arab terrorists and other supposedly imminent disclosures. McCurry was torn between providing information quickly and confirming its accuracy. "[M]y caution note to the reporters always was, 'Slow down. Let's get it right because we could easily send the story off in the wrong direction.' "[44] The insatiable twenty-four-hour news cycle, McCurry insists, was perhaps the most critical, if quotidian, challenge facing a press secretary during the 1990s.

After turbulent and mainly low public approval ratings his first two years, things began slowly to improve for President Clinton in 1995. In that year, no less than 40 percent or more of Americans told pollsters they thought the president was doing a good job, and on a few occasions—Clinton's handling of the Oklahoma City bombing, for example—that number climbed to 50 percent. And although the budget deadlock late in the year pushed his ratings downward temporarily, 1996 brought him rock-steady ratings at or above 50 percent, from which they never receded.[45]

Three factors, I would argue, resuscitated Clinton's ascent in popularity: the economic boom of the mid-1990s, the president's "triangulation" strategy of leading from the political center, and Mike McCurry. Clinton's press secretary salved the raw, strained relationship between the White House and the national press corps. According to UPI's Helen Thomas, "The first two years were almost a debacle in press relations. He knew he had to clear the air and there was a 180-degree change in the atmosphere."[46] The presence of McCurry enabled otherwise untrusting and increasingly disillusioned journalists to find something in the Democratic administration that was genuine and honorable. "If you have a popular president," noted one of McCurry's predecessors, "you're going to have a popular press secretary."[47] Though the converse is not necessarily true, there does seem to be a correlation. It was harder for writers to assail the White House when the president's point man was someone they truly liked.

McCurry's popularity and effectiveness would serve the White House well at the end of 1995. That fall, talks between the Congress and the president had stalled over the escalating budget dispute, and the two sides reached an impasse. On November 14, a partial government shutdown began and lasted a week. A month later, when President Clinton vetoed a Republican bill that included Medicare cuts and balanced-budget provisions, stalemate returned. On December 16, a second government shutdown occurred. This one would last twenty-one days, the longest in American history. On January 5, Clinton finally signed a compromise measure that featured smaller reductions in Medicare spending, as well as a seven-year, balanced-budget proposal using congressional numbers. During the standoff, the Democrats won a larger percentage of public approval than the Republicans, and their favorability ratings increased.[48] "In the game of brinksmanship," ABC's Ted Koppel later said, "it was the Democrats who were winning the public relations battle."[49]

The president's public relations success with the budget wrangle carried over into the election year, though in the unlikeliest of ways. During the winter of 1995–1996, with Washington gripped by gridlock, the country seemed to be stuck in a holding pattern. Both government shutdowns had done nothing to improve bipartisanship on the Hill or between Congress and the president. And a series of revelations about Hillary Clinton only increased the tension. During the first week of January, the White House released documents that had been requested by the Senate committee investigating Whitewater. Those materials included a memo written by David Watkins, a former White House employee, which said that the first lady wanted the travel office staff swiftly replaced or there would be "hell to pay." Mrs. Clinton had previously denied any involvement in the firings. Other documents contained sixty-hours worth of billing records from Madison Guaranty Savings & Loan, with which the first lady had said she'd been barely associated—records investigators had subpoenaed two years earlier. According to an attorney, a member of Mrs. Clinton's staff had just located the papers on the previous day, two days, incidentally, after the statute of limitations had expired.

Needless to say, many Americans were skeptical. About half the people surveyed in a Gallup poll in January said they thought Hillary Clinton was lying about Whitewater and about the travel office affair. For the first time in her four years in Washington, the first lady was actually drawing more negative than positive opinion ratings. In short, her image was in the tank.[50] Then on January 8, 1996, *New York Times* columnist William Safire wrote a column called "Blizzard of Lies," which further attacked her credibility. Safire described the contents of the recent documents and the damning significance of their late discovery: "Americans of all political persuasions are coming to the sad realization that our First Lady—a woman of undoubted talents who was a role model for many in her generation—is a congenital liar."[51] The next day, Mike McCurry relayed the president's reaction: Were he not the president, Clinton said, he would "deliver a more forceful response to the bridge of Safire's nose." Most of the press loved the statement and applauded the president's moxie. "I for one find such conduct refreshing," declared a *Chicago Sun-Times* editorial.[52] Others merely chuckled at the idea of the president duking it out with a seventy-year-old writer.[53] But most of those who were angry seemed to direct their wrath not at Clinton, but at Safire for using such venomous language in the first place, and for having the "gall" to talk about honesty when he once worked for Richard Nixon.[54] The episode seemed to snap Clinton out of his wintry lethargy and to jump-start his and his staff's confidence.

CONCLUSION

Why were Clinton's relations with the press no better than they were for much of his first term? Certainly, much of the blame must be laid at the president's door. No politician, no matter how popular, likable, or talented, can afford to exercise bad judgment or otherwise blunder in the sometimes-egregious manner that President Clinton did. His paranoid approach to damage control frequently made matters worse, and the best staff imaginable cannot be expected to vaporize every crisis to come along, or stave off negative news indefinitely. Which raises the second factor: President Clinton did not begin his term with the best staff imaginable. Far from it. Upon taking office, the president surrounded himself with many of his youthful campaign troops, electioneering strategists who were ill-equipped to serve as administrative aides. As the president later confided to strategist Dick Morris in 1995, "It's a great Cabinet. But I didn't spend the time I should have choosing my staff. I just reached out and took the people who had helped get me elected and put them on the staff. It was a mistake."[55] Though loyal and capable, people like Stephanopoulos and Myers were too green to be effective and therefore stumbled a lot before being replaced by more seasoned substitutes.

A third, yet more minor, element in Clinton's press difficulties stemmed from a slightly more jaundiced national press corps. Of course, journalists have always been labeled a more skeptical breed than the rest of the population. But in post-Watergate decades, that skepticism has become even more "facile and hypercritical."[56] It is a skepticism that tends not only to challenge politicians' opinions, but often questions their motives. And, in the 1990s, journalists added a bit more sarcasm to the attitude. *New York Times* writer Maureen Dowd's description of Clinton's 1994 return to Oxford University was a memorable example: "President Clinton returned today for a sentimental journey to the university where he didn't inhale, didn't get drafted, and didn't get a degree."[57]

An undisciplined president, an inexperienced staff, and an often irreverent press corps explain much of Clinton's poor public relations during his first term. But the quality of his staff improved considerably, and by the arrival of the 1996 campaign the White House's communications team was steaming along smoothly. Mike McCurry, in particular, seemed to have charmed a majority of Washington journalists, and for a time he managed almost single-handedly to thaw relations between the president and the press. Certainly, he served the president well; McCurry was arguably Clinton's "most valuable asset in selling his agenda to the public."[58] While the sometimes-reckless behavior of the occupant of the White House was another matter, the administration's outlook did appear promising. Besides, 1996 was a campaign year, and no one campaigned more energetically and enthusiastically than Bill Clinton.

NOTES

1. George Stephanopoulos, *All Too Human: A Political Education* (Boston: Little, Brown, 1999), p. 112.

2. Quoted in Christopher Hanson, "How to Satisfy a Spin-ster Every Time," *Columbia Journalism Review* (July/August 1998), p. 17.

3. Quoted in Tim Graham, *Pattern of Deception: The Media's Role in the Clinton Presidency* (Alexandria, VA: Media Research Center, 1996), p. 118.

4. Quoted in ABC News, *Nightline*, "The Clinton Years" (January 9, 2001).

5. Thomas M. DeFrank, "Call Him Prof. Stephanopoulos," *New York Daily News* (December 4, 1996), p. 8.

6. The Greek analogy is Lloyd Grove's. Grove, "The White House Kiddie Corps," *Washington Post* (June 1, 1993), p. C1.

7. Peter A. Jay, "The Rise and Fall of Women in the Clinton White House," *Baltimore Sun* (April 11, 1996), p. A13.

8. Ian Brodie, "Former Aide Accuses Clinton of Operating Club for 'White Boys,' " *London Times* (April 10, 1996).

9. Bill Nichols, "Laughter and Emotion Mark Myers' Last Day," *USA Today* (December 23, 1994), p. A4.

10. Mark C. Barabak, "Dee Dee Myers Enjoying Fruits of Stint as Clinton Press Secretary," *San Diego Union-Tribune* (June 11, 1995), p. A3.

11. Stephanopoulos, *All Too Human*, p. 137.

12. By the end of his second term, some assessments were more positive. In November 2000, historian Douglas Brinkley called Clinton "probably our finest orator as President since Kennedy. He delivered dozens of dazzling speeches. But all of that oratorical emotion and showmanship will dissipate over time, and what will be remembered is the clip of his finger wagging." Brinkley, quoted in Jay Branegan, "What We'll Remember," *Time* 156 (November 30, 2000), p. 94. Brinkley's statement ought to read with the following caveat: the oratorical standard for twentieth-century presidents in the postwar era is fairly low.

13. David E. Procter and Kurt Ritter, "Inaugurating the Clinton Presidency: Regenerative Rhetoric and the American Community," in Robert E. Denton, Jr., and Rachel L. Holloway (eds.), *The Clinton Presidency: Images, Issues, and Communication Strategies* (Westport, CT: Praeger Publishers, 1996), p. 13. For more on Clinton's gifts as an extemporaneous speaker, see Dick Morris, *Behind the Oval Office: Winning the Presidency in the Nineties* (New York: Random House, 1997), pp. 120–21.

14. Woodrow Wilson, the first president to hold press conferences regularly, also initially kept an ambitious regimen: He gave two a week for almost two years, and one a week for six months, before virtually abandoning the practice altogether; in his last term he gave only four. Contemporary presidents have at least shown more consistency. "Presidents Reagan and Nixon averaged only one every two months, Reagan because he hated the preparation, Nixon because he

hated the press." William Safire, "Question Time," *New York Times* (February 15, 2001), p. A31.

15. Fitzwater, interview with Tim Russert, CNBC News (March 13, 1999).

16. Robert E. Denton, Jr., and Rachel L. Holloway, "Clinton and the Town Hall Meetings: Mediated Conversation and the Risk of Being In Touch,' " in Robert E. Denton, Jr., and Rachel L. Holloway (eds.), *The Clinton Presidency: Images, Issues, and Conversation Strategies* (Westport, CT: Praeger Publishers, 1996), p. 37; Rita K. Whitlock, "The Compromising Clinton: Images of Failure, A Record of Success," in ibid., p. 126.

17. Howard Kurtz, *Spin Cycle: Inside the Clinton Propaganda Machine* (New York: Free Press, 1998), p. xxiv.

18. Graham, *Pattern of Deception*, p. 9.

19. James Stewart, *Blood Sport: The President and His Adversaries* (New York: Simon & Schuster, 1996; Touchstone, 1997), p. 34.

20. Ibid., pp. 39–40.

21. Rachel L. Holloway, "The Clintons and the Health Care Crisis: Opportunity Lost, Promise Unfulfilled," in Denton and Holloway (eds.), *The Clinton Presidency*, pp. 176–77.

22. Lydia Saad, "Public Has Cold Feet on Health Care Reform," *Gallup Poll Monthly* 347 (August 1994), p. 2.

23. Quoted in Bob Woodward, *Shadow: Five Presidents and the Legacy of Watergate* (New York: Simon & Schuster, 1999), p. 257.

24. Stewart, *Blood Sport*, p. 354; Stephanopoulos, *All Too Human*, pp. 226–28.

25. Stewart, *Blood Sport*, pp. 446–47.

26. David W. Moore and Lydia Saad, "President Clinton and the Public: A Midterm Report," *Gallup Poll Monthly* 354 (March 1995), p. 2.

27. Douglas Jehl, "A Last Briefing for Clinton Press Secretary," *New York Times* (December 23, 1994), p. A22.

28. Ken Auletta, Interview of Lloyd Cutler, "On the President and the Press," *Columbia Journalism Review* (November/December 1994), p. 45.

29. Quoted by John Anthony Maltese, "The New Media and the Lure of the Clinton Scandal," in *The Clinton Scandal and the Future of American Government*, ed. Mark J. Rozell and Clyde Wilcox (Washington, D.C.: Georgetown University Press, 2000), p. 199.

30. Carl M. Cannon and Nelson Schwartz, "Clinton's Fourth Spokesman in Two Years," *Baltimore Sun* (January 7, 1995), p. A2.

31. Ann DeVroy, " 'The Price of These Two Years Was High,' Myers Says as She Exits," *Washington Post* (December 23, 1994), p. A1.

32. For an account of this episode, see Christopher Matthews, "Dee Dee Myers Is a Hero for Our Time," *Houston Chronicle* (October 6, 1994), p. A28; and John M. Broder, "Myers Says She's Leaving White House at End of Year," *Los Angeles Times* (December 17, 1994), p. A20.

33. See, for example, Suzanne Fields, "The Whining of Dee Dee Myers," *Atlanta Journal-Constitution* (December 29, 1994), p. A10.

34. McCurry, quoted in Carl M. Cannon, "A Flack Who Uses a Smile," *Baltimore Sun* (May 19, 1996), p. E1.

35. Ibid.

36. Ibid.

37. Susan Baer, "McCurry Leaves with Reputation, Humor Intact," *Baltimore Sun* (October 2, 1998), p. A3; Helen Thomas is quoted in Carl M. Cannon, "A Flack Who Uses a Smile," *Baltimore Sun* (May 19, 1996), p. E1.

38. For example, Jerry terHorst, press secretary to President Ford. Sperling, "If Press Secretaries Had a Hall of Fame," *Christian Science Monitor* (November 19, 1996), p. 19.

39. Douglas Turner, "Good Spin Deserves Another as Clinton's Media Massage Passes from Expert to Master," *Buffalo News* (September 27, 1999), p. B2.

40. Godfrey Sperling, "If Press Secretaries Had a Hall of Fame," *Christian Science Monitor* (November 19, 1996), p. 19.

41. Braver, quoted in Judy Keen, "With Words and Wit, McCurry Makes His Mark," *USA Today* (May 4, 1995), p. A12.

42. McCurry, interview, CNN, *Reliable Sources* (August 7, 1999).

43. McCurry, interview, CNBC, *Tim Russert* (March 13, 1999).

44. Ibid.

45. Lydia Saad and Frank Newport, "Pendulum Swings Back toward Clinton," *Gallup Poll Monthly* 365 (February 1996), pp. 7–8; Frank Newport, "Clinton Maintains High Job Approval Ratings throughout Tumultuous Week," *Gallup Poll Monthly* 395 (August 1998), p. 12.

46. Thomas, quoted in Susan Baer, "Clinton Spokesman Has the Last Word," *Baltimore Sun* (July 24, 1998), p. A1.

47. The quote is from Ford press secretary Ron Nessen. Interview, CNN, *Larry King Live* (March 24, 1998).

48. David W. Moore, "Budget Dispute Helps Democrats," *Gallup Poll Monthly* 362 (November 1995), p. 10.

49. Koppel, "The Clinton Years," ABC, *Nightline* (January 1, 2001).

50. Frank Newport, "First Lady a Growing Liability for Clinton," *Gallup Poll Monthly* 364 (January 1996), p. 2.

51. William Safire, "Blizzard of Lies," *New York Times* (January 8, 1996), p. A27.

52. "President's Anger Shows He's Human," *Chicago Sun-Times* (January 14, 1996), p. A36.

53. Bill Tammeus, "You Know It's a Good Column When the President Threatens to Punch You Out," *Kansas City Star* (January 26, 1996), p. C5; Jesse E. Todd, Jr., "Let's You and Them Fight," *Baltimore Sun* (January 21, 1996), p. E7.

54. John Head, "A Writer's Right," *Atlanta Journal and Constitution* (January 19, 1996), p. A18.

55. Quoted by Dick Morris, *Behind the Oval Office*, pp. 97–98.

56. Thomas Patterson, *Out of Order* (New York: Alfred A. Knopf, 1993), p. 18.

57. Quoted in Paul Starobin, "A Generation of Vipers," *Columbia Journalism Review* (March/April 1995), p. 27.

58. Peter Baker and Howard Kurtz, "McCurry Exit: A White House Wit's End," *Washington Post* (July 24, 1998), p. A1.

3

President Clinton and the First Amendment

INTRODUCTION

In contemporary American life, the Democratic Party has become known as the party most receptive to liberal values—the party, that is, most often associated with the welfare of minorities and women, with the sympathies of "the working stiff and the reformer," and the party most hospitable to civil liberties, the Bill of Rights generally, and the First Amendment in particular.[1] That reputation was not always secure. For much of the twentieth century, Southern Democrats ensured their careers by keeping blacks away from the polls and quietly in "their place." During World War I, a Democratic president, Woodrow Wilson, gave his blessing to the most repressive censorship laws since the Alien and Sedition Acts of 1798. The party's image as defender of the Bill of Rights is relatively recent, then. But even through the 1980s it was firmly intact, with George Bush running squarely against Michael Dukakis in the 1988 presidential election atop the charge that the latter was a "card-carrying member of the A.C.L.U. [American Civil Liberties Union]." After the presidency of William Jefferson Clinton, however, Americans may no longer make the connection.

Of course, Bill Clinton did not get to the White House by trumpeting an unmistakably liberal agenda. "Most liberals knew this," recalls George Stephanopolous, "[and] understood that Clinton wasn't really one of us.

But it felt good to get lost in the partisan reverie, to be carried back to a time when photos of FDR graced Democratic mantels like the icons of a patron saint, a time when the Kennedy brothers epitomized the best and the brightest, a time long before McGovern, Carter, Mondale, and Dukakis were caricatured into a sadly comic Mount Rushmore, symbols of a party out of touch and doomed to defeat. It felt good, again, to think about winning.[2]

Clinton rose to power as a centrist, a moderate, someone able to graft the most popular Republican ideas onto the Democratic platform, and then lead from the middle. Rather than assume responsibility for a generous interpretation of individual rights, he emphasized the need for stricter adherence to the greater communal good. In this worldview, community trumps individuality. And therefore he was quick to enact tougher crime laws and push "decency" legislation. The result has not been pretty. Legal eagle Alan Dershowitz, who says he had supported Bill Clinton "despite, not because of, his record in protecting the Bill of Rights," summarized liberals' frustration with the president in 1998:

Virtually every protection of the Bill of Rights has been diminished under the Presidency of the man who, as governor, opposed Robert Bork's nomination to the Supreme Court on the grounds that Bork's 'constitutional theories of individual and civil rights' constituted a 'threat.' Yet he has turned out to be the presidential equivalent of a judicial Robert Bork on some of these same issues of individual rights.[3]

President Clinton's own choice of judges did not impress people concerned about individual rights. "Think a Democratic President guarantees progressive judicial nominees?" asks John Nichols of *The Progressive*. "Think again."[4] Political scientists and judicial experts who have compared twentieth-century presidents place Clinton alongside the likes of Gerald Ford and just barely above Richard Nixon.[5] Clinton's aversion to appointing strong liberal judges has caused some critics to believe the president was actually "biased" against liberals. "He just thinks they will cause him political trouble, so he won't appoint any," says California judge Stephen Reinhardt.[6] Civil libertarian Nat Hentoff agrees: "When it comes to court appointments, it's like everything else with Clinton— he has no principles whatsoever. . . . If he thought it would make him more popular, he'd appoint Caligula."[7]

Bill Clinton, as most people know, had a passion for testing possible positions with public polls. He liked to be behind public opinion, or else just slightly ahead of it and with advance knowledge that it was likely to follow. As a result, his record on such unpopular causes as the rights of criminal suspects or of Internet pornographers disheartened libertarians. Alan Dershowitz writes that when he heard Clinton's 1998 State of the Union address he cheered—until the president began talking about the need to preserve the original Bill of Rights document. "[T]he symbolism was grating. Here was the President—who had done more to destroy the values reflected in the Bill of Rights than any President in recent memory—shedding crocodile tears about an old piece of paper."[8]

How did Clinton try to "destroy" those values? And to what issues was Dershowitz referring? Mainly to the First, Fourth, and Seventh Amendments, which together encompass basic civil rights ranging from freedom of speech to privacy protections to habeas corpus procedures. With but a few exceptions, Clinton's record on Bill of Rights-related controversies proved deeply disappointing. With respect to the First Amendment, Bill Clinton certainly never promised to be a champion of free speech but a spokesperson for workers, parents, and families. That is why in 1999, less than two months after the Columbine massacre in Littleton, Colorado, the president announced an investigation of Hollywood violence. That is also why, six months later, the administration tried to convince the Supreme Court that a federal law forcing cable companies to use improved scrambling technology was constitutional. Neither of these efforts was particularly controversial. Other than making studio executives squirm a little and aggravating cable company managers, the White House had found small-potato projects for which there was substantial public approval, little or no press criticism, and virtually no political fallout.[9]

President Clinton took on bigger game, too, and not always with predictible results. While he sometimes supported encroachments into free-speech protection, he also occasionally safeguarded them. In 1997, constitutional lawyer Floyd Abrams concluded dourly that Clinton seemed not to care: "Time and again, the Administration has opposed serious First Amendment claims in court, acquiesced in serious First Amendment damage by legislation and ignored First Amendment limits in its own conduct."[10] Yet, Abrams lumps campaign-finance reform in with other threats, even though it is certainly debatable whether money is expression and not property.

Abrams also fails to give Clinton credit for other actions. In one of his few departures from popular causes, the president took a braver stand on the issue of flag burning. Bill Clinton vetoed a bill that would have altered the First Amendment itself in order to make burning the American flag a crime. Efforts to protect the flag go back a long way in the United States, as far back as the revolutionary period. For most of the twentieth century, too, laws have existed both on the state and federal level to punish people who abuse, burn, or otherwise desecrate the flag. Then, in 1989, the Supreme Court ruled that burning a flag was an expression of speech that could not be prohibited. The ruling essentially upended all state and federal flag-desecration laws. One year later, the Court was faced with a new federal measure outlawing flag burning, and once again a majority ruled such statutes unconstitutional. The five-to-four decision stimulated even further discussion about steps to protect the flag, but none came to fruition until the mid-1990s when Congress passed an amendment to the First Amendment banning such action.

The flag-burning amendment proved a short-lived issue, which seemed to pass in and out of the media unusually quickly. This was not the case with two other firestorms. In the 1990s, as in most other times, these controversies involved perceived threats to public decency and to national security.

THE QUEST FOR DECENCY

The election year 1996 produced a wave of proposals for "decency" legislation. Concerns about cable television programming and Internet pornography topped the list of America's cultural anxieties. And considering that Republicans had trounced Democrats two years before in the midterm 1994 elections, President Clinton could not afford to give the political opposition any ammunition. Polls told the president that the American people regarded him as a liberal, a failed liberal who, early on, had lost and been embarrassed in his campaign to defend gays in the military and then to promote the health care plan his wife supervised. Some thought, political consultant Dick Morris chief among them, that President Clinton had to recapture the political center. To do that, he latched onto Morris's "triangulation" strategy of tiptoeing the line between both parties, and so it was that Clinton eventually signed off on such Republican-initiated enterprises as welfare reform, and endorsed "decency" legislation.[11] What Clinton did, in other words, was to embrace the by-now stale Republican refrain of "family values." When he did that, he effectively jeopardized what some consider to be the most sacred of the Bill of Rights, the First Amendment. "No part of our Constitution is less family-friendly than the First Amendment," Floyd

Abrams wrote in 1997. "None is more hostile to government. . . . It is counterintuitive enough for any Administration to be genuinely protective of the First Amendment. For Bill Clinton's Administration, it has been impossible."[12]

In January 1996, for example, Clinton signed the Military Honor and Decency Act, which prohibited American military bases around the world from selling explicit sexual publications like *Penthouse*. Not even the Defense Department was convinced of the law's constitutionality, and before long a federal judge confirmed that it did not, in fact, meet that standard. The judge argued sharply that American citizens "do not jettison their constitutional rights simply by enlisting in the armed forces." Ironically, the judge in this case, Shira Scheindlin, was appointed by Bill Clinton himself. Other opportunities for passing comparable "decency" legislation arose soon enough, though, and attracted far more support.

To be sure, many Americans in the 1990s were worried that the nation's popular culture was spinning out of control, that standards of civility and propriety were rapidly vanishing. What, for example, should be done about Internet web sites devoted to scenes of sadomasochism? Was it permissible for cable companies to broadcast graphic programming during prime-time hours? How could parents, so strapped by the demands of dual careers, supervise children with access to these images? Of course, as Abrams observed, the First Amendment was not designed with families in mind.[13] But such a perspective would hardly have assuaged a restless majority of Americans. The Telecommunications Reform Act (TRA), therefore, was the signature bill of a public troubled by the growth of new technologies and new media, along with their accompanying spread of violence and obscenity. Part of the legislation called for telephone deregulation, while the rest, under the Communications Decency Act (CDA) pertained to television and the Internet. Sponsored by Nebraska Democrat James Exon, the measure's two most famous passages provided for installation of V-chips in televisions in order to block out offending material, and banned the transmission of "indecent" material to children over the Internet. Both provisions were geared to protect minors with access to such fare, even though they also penalized adults. The House of Representatives passed the bill on February 1, 1996 by a vote of 414 to sixteen. The same day, the Senate passed it ninety-one to five. "A bipartisan attack on the First Amendment," one writer said.[14] And one week later, the president signed it into law.

Clinton's most publicized foray into cyberspace regulation provoked considerable opposition. Organizations denouncing the law included the American Library Association, the Society for Professional Journalists, the American Civil Liberties Union, and Microsoft. The ACLU convinced a judge in Philadelphia to stop enforcement of the CDA on the grounds that it not only failed to define what decency was but also effectively lowered the standard for permissible content for adults. In presenting the case against the Communications Decency Act, appellate attorney Bruce Ennis summarized the law's likely impact: "Our strongest argument is that this law will have the unconstitutional effect of banning indecent speech from adults in all of cyberspace. For forty years, this Court has repeatedly and unanimously ruled that Government cannot constitutionally reduce the adult population to reading and viewing only what is appropriate for children. That is what this law does."[15] "You want to smite smut," Daniel Schorr chimed on National Public Radio, "smite smut some other way, but not by withholding it from adults [as if] kids can't see it."[16] Wendy Kaminer, writing in *The Nation*, said the problem with the bill was that its framers had it precisely backward: "The . . . Act prohibited indecency on the Internet while easing restrictions on media mergers. It's the perfect example of what not to do. Progressives should be demanding a regulated marketplace; as for speech—laissez faire."[17] In the media, relatively less attention was paid to television V-chips than to the Internet. Presumably, many Americans felt less threatened by parental-friendly technology that could be used or not used as adults so desired. The Internet provision raised hackles, however, in part because of the bill's vagueness, in part because of its ultimate unenforceability, but also in part because of the medium's novelty and the techno-utopian attitude many Americans had toward it.

The fight over the Internet not only raised the usual disputes over what indecency, obscenity, and pornography are, but what type of medium the Internet itself was. Tech writer Charlie Simpson captured the dilemma perfectly: "Is the Internet a broadcast media that is subject to legislation and government imposed restrictions? Is it a print media like this magazine which enjoys the constitutional protection of the First Amendment? Or, is it something in between, or altogether different? Is it protected under privacy acts, or is it open to public display much like electronic graffiti?"[18] What about the traditional criterion of "community standards" that judicial examinations of obscenity routinely invoke? George Will wisely noted that the country was wrestling with a "technology . . . that renders obsolete the vocabulary that's been used in prior First Amendment cases."[19] The Internet's very novelty seemed to encourage both defenders and critics toward dogmatic positions, but by emphasizing "children" as a beneficiary of the bill, supporters of the Communications Decency Act had successfully driven a wedge in the body politic. Within four years, though, libertarians had identified the new medium as the most important battleground for free expression. "The independence of the Internet becomes the newest test of a government's will to encourage and sustain a free press."[20]

The Supreme Court struck down the law on June 27, 1997, by a count of seven to two. The justices concluded that the law was too vague and would thus exert "a chilling effect on free speech." The ruling was greeted with a combination of delight and relief by many in the media. One observer believed that the Court showed itself "considerably more educated on Internet and PC technology and issues than that of Congress."[21] Perhaps the president was already reconsidering, too. Ironically, he told an international audience assembled in Bonn a week later that governments ought to keep their hands off Internet content.[22] Michael Kinsley, writing for *Time*, said he supported the Supreme Court decision—"the Webbies are basically in the right"—but admitted the issue was a thorny one for any parent: "Freedom suddenly costs more in terms of the competing values. I still side with freedom, but it's dishonest not to acknowledge that the price has gone up."[23]

Internet censorship was by no means over, however. In October 1998, Congress passed the Child Online Protection Act with President Clinton's support. This "offspring of the ill-conceived Communications Decency Act," as one writer termed it, was supposed to get around the constitutional hazards of 1996–1997 by focusing on commercial web sites and by emphasizing "child protection."[24] It didn't work. In February 1999, a federal judge in Philadelphia ordered a preliminary injunction against the act on the grounds that it encroached on protected speech for adults. By the summer of that year, the administration seemed more content to allow private-sector filtering technology to remedy the problem. Commerce Secretary William Daley declared in July that services such as GetNetWise, which provide parental resources on the Web, demonstrate "that not every problem with the Internet needs a legislative solution."[25]

NATIONAL SECURITY BILL

In the wake of a scandal in 1999 over allegations of Chinese espionage, there arose frequent cries in the media about the need for tightened national security. Whether nuclear scientist Wen Ho Lee was guilty of anything more than sloppiness or eccentric behavior, the perception that America's guard was down abounded. Pundits and politicians, especially Republican ones, fulminated about the White House's looking the other way while other countries seemingly stole our nuclear secrets. The president and his Democratic cohorts appeared too focused on foreign political contributions, while the rest of the nation paid more attention to Wall Street. Prosperity in general and the end of the cold war had led us into a false sense of safety. Now was the time to shore up our defenses. With that mentality, two Republican congressmen and intelligence committee chairmen—Senator Richard Shelby of Alabama and Representative Porter Goss of Florida—wrote a Central Intelligence Agency (CIA)-inspired bill to punish individuals who willingly divulged classified government information. Officials who gave out such unauthorized information to reporters would be subject to jail and fines, which would obviously have stifled news gathering in a place like Washington. In such a climate, who would dare talk to the press "if a slip of the tongue might mean up to three years at Lompoc, California—if they were lucky—or the maximum security pen at Marion, Illinois—if they were not"?[26]

The bill was not altogether rotten. It contained provisions requiring the government to reform its bloated classification system. Senator Daniel Patrick Moynihan had devoted several years' work to these provisions, which would fall by the wayside if the bill failed in Congress. Too bad, said the press in a virtual chorus. "As much as we want to see the commission's [reforms] enacted into law," declared the *Buffalo News*, "we cannot support an assault on the freedoms that this country was built upon. The bill's reach is too broad, and it deserves a veto."[27]

Pointing out that anti-espionage laws were already in place to prosecute such people, columnist William Safire expressed his disbelief: "Can this be happening in America? Are we about to adopt the sort of 'Official Secrets Act' that lets British officials decide what news is suitable for the public?"[28] The title of Safire's column, "The Secrecy Legacy," seemed almost like the *New York Times*'s challenge to President Clinton not to be remembered this way. Having been criticized for becoming weak-kneed on other First Amendment fracases, the *New York Times* seemed to make a point of pressuring President Clinton on this particular one.[29] With Safire out in front, the paper sounded the alarm, even scored that year's presidential candidates for failing to take stronger stands on the issue. Safire ended his last column on the subject on this gloomy note: "They'll leave this systematic squelching of criticism to Clinton, probably hoping he signs this un-American abomination and slams the White House door after him."[30]

Clinton did not. Warning that bills of that type could "chill legitimate activities that are at the heart of a democracy," the president vetoed the measure. Journalists welcomed the move. "We meet enough obstacles that are meant to keep our wrongs a secret," wrote one. "Let's not add another one to that list."[31] The *Los Angeles Times* exclaimed that Clinton had "preserved the First Amendment" with this single act.[32] On December 27, 2000, President Clinton signed a new version of the bill that did not carry the felony provision for disclosures. It was one of the president's few bright spots during his last, turbulent days in office. It was also one of the president's few efforts on behalf of the First Amendment.

CONCLUSION

Clinton's cool attitude toward freedom of speech represents a modern Democratic compromise. Thirty years ago, America's libertarian landscape was notably different, remarks Stuart Taylor, Jr. In the 1960s, amid the heyday of such landmark court cases as *New York Times v. Sullivan*, "threats to the freedoms of speech . . . came mainly from the Right, and the First Amendment's champions were crusading liberals such as [Justice William] Brennan. Not so now. Uninhibited free speech has gone out of fashion in liberal circles—in the Clinton Administration, in Congress, in state and local governments, at the most prestigious universities, and at the best cocktail parties."[33] Was Taylor right about the Clinton administration? The answer is that the Clinton record is mixed or "tepid" at best.[34] Certainly, for an old-style liberal Democrat, the record is disappointing, yet Clinton's First Amendment stances remind us that he is not and never was an old-style liberal Democrat. According to Floyd Abrams, for example, President Clinton has tried "more than any other [administration] since Richard Nixon's . . . to affect the content of what appears on television."[35] Not that the president has favored unpopular legislation, but he is certainly no liberal. And in most ways he is actually less a centrist than a populist. For most populists, the press is generally important, yet in a new-media universe, Bill Clinton has been able to minimize the influence of traditional forums. Clinton never liked journalists much anyway—they'd burned him in 1992, and sometimes hounded him over the Whitewater investigation, the travel office mess, Federal Bureau of Investigation (FBI) files, and the like. A veteran survivor of numerous scandal wars, the president had met the enemy and thought it looked a lot like the otherwise well-meaning journalists who covered him for a living. Rather than pay homage to the press, then, or to ideological prizes such as the principle of freedom of speech, he bowed only to the power of public opinion polls. In any case, he viewed First Amendment issues primarily from the perspective of a pragmatic politician whose first concern was to get the most votes.

Despite Clinton's endorsement in 1996 of a whole repressive chamber of horrors, his First Amendment record actually improved thereafter, though libertarians critical of his first-term actions seem unwilling to qualify their earlier harsh assessments. Abrams, who admits voting for someone other than Clinton (or Bush) in 1992 because he believed him "thoroughly manipulative and dishonest," has not, that I can tell, publicly praised Clinton for his veto of the national security bill of 2000.[36] He did say after the 1992 election that he expected Clinton to clash with the press, but virtually all presidents have had their quarrels with journalists, so that is hardly a venturesome statement.[37]

NOTES

1. Michael Kelly, "Clinton's Legacy," *Washington Post* (October 30, 1997), p. A23. Of course, not all self-described liberals today revere the First Amendment. In fact, a few have renounced it, while others are in the process of reconsidering their allegiance. Ronald K. L. Collins and David M. Skover, for example, call "much current First Amendment law . . . anti-democratic." Collins and Skover, in "Speech & Power: Is First Amendment Absolutism Obsolete? A Nation Forum," *The Nation* 265 (July 21, 1997). According to Floyd Abrams, they do so simply because the "wrong" people are protected by it. Floyd Abrams, in ibid.; and Abrams, "Look Who's Trashing the First Amendment," *Columbia Journalism Review* (November/December 1997), p. 53.

2. George Stephanopoulos, *All Too Human: A Political Education* (Boston: Little, Brown and Co., 1999), p. 47.

3. Alan M. Dershowitz, *Sexual McCarthyism: Clinton, Starr, and the Emerging Constitutional Crisis* (New York: Basic Books, 1998), p. 152.

4. John Nichols, "The Clinton Courts: Liberals Need Not Apply," *The Progressive* 60 (September 1, 1996), p. 25.

5. Nichols cites such scholars as Ronald Stidham and Michael Gerhardt. Ibid.

6. Stephen Reinhardt, quoted in John Nichols, "The Clinton Courts," ibid.

7. Nat Hentoff, quoted in John Nichols, "The Clinton Courts," ibid.

8. Dershowitz, *Sexual McCarthyism*, p. 149.

9. Amy Wallace and Faye Fiore, "Hollywood Surprised by Clinton's Vio-

lence Inquiry," *Los Angeles Times* (June 7, 1999), p. A1; Linda Greenhouse, "U.S. Seeks to Restore Limits on Cable Sex Programming," *New York Times* (December 1, 1999), p. A19.

10. Floyd Abrams, "Clinton Versus the First Amendment," *New York Times* (March 30, 1997), VI, p. 42.

11. Dick Morris, *Behind the Oval Office: Winning the Presidency in the Nineties* (New York: Random House, 1997), pp. 80–84.

12. Ibid.

13. Ibid.

14. Bill Hough, letter, *Communications Week* (September 9, 1996), np.

15. Quoted in "Communications Decency Act: Gone but Not Forgotten," *Online Newsletter* (September 1, 1997).

16. Daniel Schorr, National Public Radio, *Weekend Edition* (June 28, 1997).

17. Wendy Kaminer, in "Speech & Power: Is First Amendment Absolutism Obsolete? A Nation Forum," *The Nation* 265 (July 21, 1997), p. 15.

18. Charlie Simpson, "Crossing the Lines Online," *Digital Age* 15 (April 1, 1996), p. 6.

19. George Will, ABC, *This Week* (June 29, 1997).

20. Leonard Sussman, quoted in "Internet Censorship Threatens Free Press—Report," *Reuters* (April 26, 2000).

21. "Communications Decency Act: Gone but Not Forgotten," *Online Newsletter* (September 1, 1997).

22. Clinton Wilder, "Spotlight—Clinton: Hands Off E-Commerce," *Information Week* (June 30, 1997), p. 32.

23. Michael Kinsley, "Attention, Web Mart Shoppers!" *Time* (November 17, 1997), p. 114.

24. "Policing Cyberspace," *The Nation* 268 (March 1, 1999), p. 4.

25. "Internet Industry Unveils Parent Protection Program," *Communications Daily* 19 (July 30, 1999).

26. David Wise, "The Nation/The C.I.A.: The Secrecy Police Will Be Back Soon," *Los Angeles Times* (December 10, 2000), p. M2.

27. "Secrecy and Freedom," *Buffalo News* (November 3, 2000), p. B20.

28. William Safire, "The Secrecy Legacy," *New York Times* (November 2, 2000), p. A31.

29. The *National Journal* referred to the *Times*'s editorial page as "formerly a guardian of First Amendment rights." "Boy Scouts v. Gays," *National Journal* 32 (September 9, 2000), p. 2769.

30. Ibid.

31. Monica D. Morales, "Clinton Vetoes Bill That Would Limit Journalists' Powers," *The Lariat* (November 9, 2000), np.

32. David Wise, "The Nation/The C.I.A.," p. M2.

33. Stuart Taylor, Jr., "How Liberals Got Tired of the Freedom of Speech," *National Journal* 32 (October 14, 2000), p. 3224.

34. Abrams, "Clinton Versus the First Amendment," p. 42.

35. Ibid.

36. Quoted in Scott Stephens, "Village Voice Talks at College, Hentoff Airs Views of Schott, Clinton," *Cleveland Plain Dealer* (February 12, 1993), p. B1.

37. Thom Gross, "Conflict with Press 'Inevitable,' " *St. Louis Post-Dispatch* (November 13, 1992), p. A8.

4

Campaign '96

INTRODUCTION

The pressure was on Bill Clinton for his second presidential campaign. His popularity had edged up slightly during the government shutdowns, but overall his job approval ratings had taken a beating since his 1993 inauguration. The new Republican-controlled Congress was pushing him into a political corner, and special counsels were busy looking into his and his wife's Whitewater dealings, his administration's travel office practices, and its mishandling of FBI files. In addition, Paula Jones was pursuing her lawsuit against the president for alleged sexual harassment while he was governor of Arkansas and she a state employee. Without question, Bill Clinton was the most investigated—and some might say likewise "harassed"—president in American history. Even more than the lawsuit and the special counsel investigations, however, the president was troubled by his political fortunes in the upcoming election year. Voters had already sent a clear message in 1994, electing Republican majorities in the House and Senate for the first time in four decades. Clinton's first four years in office had simply not gone well. They had been marked by weakness and disorganization, by failure and tragedy. His image as a leader remained seriously in question. Though the economy was starting to pick up and actually hum, Clinton had few solid administrative achievements about which to boast, and Congress seemed

on the verge of making the president irrelevant with its ferocious legislative agenda. "February and March [of 1995] were truly the Gingrich
administration," one White House adviser recalled, referring to the new
Republican Speaker of the House.[1] Worse, Clinton had presided over
some spectacular debacles—the Health Care Reform Bill of 1994 being
the premier example—which made him look incompetent or lost.

The president was therefore taking no chances. He consulted with his
longtime political partner, guerilla adviser Dick Morris, the man who
had helped him plot an earlier comeback after then-Governor Clinton
lost his first reelection bid in 1980. Clinton had also turned to Morris
for help in 1992, but Morris recommended James Carville instead, citing
a prior commitment and later confessing his doubts as to Clinton's
chances. In 1994, however, Morris was eager to be of service, excited
about the prospect of becoming a presidential confidant, and filled with
ideas about innovative executive leadership.

Morris urged Clinton to find "a third way," one distinctive from the
Republican and Democratic platforms but no mere compromise straight
down the middle either. As he later explained it, this strategy of "triangulation" strategy did contain direction and purpose, but it involved
"tacking" rather than sailing blindly against the wind.[2] Above all, the
politically independent Morris advised, the president needed to respect
the opposition. "So what we must do is to relieve the frustrations that
impelled the election of the Republican Congress in 1994 by helping to
address the issues on which they ran."[3] Clinton was receptive. For almost
two years, from September 1994 to August 1996, Morris counseled the
president. So worried were the two men about political recrimination
from fellow Democrats and about territorial squabbling within the White
House, that for the first seven months of the alliance they kept Morris's
role secret, speaking mainly on the telephone and using the code name
"Charlie" for the president's new stealth-adviser.[4]

Dick Morris's "triangulation" strategy may have been pragmatic, but
it was hardly designed to inspire gratitude on the part of liberals. "Its
classic pitfalls," explained Christopher Hitchens, "are the accusations that
fall between zig and zag. Its classic advantage is the straight plea for the
benefit of the 'lesser evils' calculus, which in most modern elections
means a straight and preconditioned choice between one and another, or
A and B, or Tweedledum and Tweedledee."[5] After the Republican land-
slide of '94, however, Clinton was desperate. Accordingly, the president
decided to make key concessions to the 104th Congress and even to
conservative Republicans in general. He declared the era of big govern-

ment over in his State of the Union address. He signed "decency" legislation, welfare reform, and the Defense of Marriage Act, all of which
were normally anathema to the Democratic Party. Clinton, the new Democrat, was pulling out the rug from under the Republicans.

For their part, though, the Republicans were steadily pulling the rug
out from under themselves by nominating for the presidency Bob Dole,
the bland, seventy-three-year-old Senate majority leader from Kansas.
Dole was respected and experienced, a venerable party loyalist in line
to collect after a lifetime of service. But he generated no excitement
among the public, the press, or other politicians. Most people who said
they planned to vote for Dole indicated that what they were really doing
was voting *against* Bill Clinton. Frustrated Republicans complained that
Dole was the victim of a liberal press and simply hoped for the best in
November.

How did the media cover the 1996 presidential election? What sorts
of issues did journalists and pundits focus on? Did they demonstrate a
bias in favor of one candidate over the other? Did the so-called new
media of 1992 make a comparably significant contribution to the campaign? To answer these questions, it is necessary first to address one
political reality in 1996: The president early on captured a substantial
lead over his Republican challenger and maintained it almost until the
end. That double-digit cushion took away much of the drama, interest,
and speculation a closer race would otherwise have elicited. Therefore,
journalists and the public alike seemed considerably more subdued than
they had in 1992, when a stumbling incumbent, a surging upstart, and
the novelty and popularity of a hot third candidate kept the whole country
guessing. In 1996, politics made fewer headlines and inspired fewer editorials. With the economy picking up steam and the outcome of the race
seemingly a foregone conclusion, America paid less attention to the campaign. For those people who did, says one scholar, "the tumult and shout-
ing were mostly contrived."[6]

GENERAL COMMENTARY

The national media paid less attention to the 1996 presidential campaign than they had to the race in 1992. According to some estimates,
in fact, coverage of the campaign was down 40 percent from the previous
four years.[7] Why? Robert Lichter, of the Center for Media and Public
Affairs, listed the missing ingredients in October: "This race lacks the
things that really get journalists salivating—a good horse race, candi-

dates bunched closely together, a lot of conflict. Bill Clinton is not attacking Bob Dole, and Dole has surprisingly not done much attacking
on Clinton. No really juicy scandals."[8] Lichter's comments appeared on
the CNN Sunday program *Reliable Sources*. On the same program, the
show's host, Bernard Kalb, discussed the situation with journalist Martin
Schram:

Kalb: The media seemed bored by the campaign. Is that something of an irresponsible luxury, Marty?

Schram: Oh, it sure is, Bernie. I mean, look at *Newsweek*. *Newsweek* asked the
question, is it over? And then what happens, then they wonder why the public
is bored, why the public is not enthused, why the public is telling pollsters
they're not enthused. It's irresponsible for anyone—newsmagazine, or anyone
else to first of all start prejudging is it over? Cover the campaign. Don't try to
get out in front of it.[9]

All the panelists on the program agreed that desperate though the media
were for some old-fashioned political combat, the candidates just weren't
biting. The media had not even been able to get controversial issues like
abortion or affirmative action on the table. "So the campaign," Howard
Kurtz concluded, "isn't really about anything other than the tactical shifts
in the ads."[10]

Yet, even that was not always possible. On the national scene, there
was sometimes less to chew on for grazing journalists. Sophisticated
computer programs, for example, told the candidates precisely in which
areas of the country they were weakest, strongest, or most vulnerable to
sudden shifts. Therefore, political ads had become not only state-targeted
but microdemographically selective. Of course, political finance strategists have always had to exercise judicious use of campaign dollars, but
now technology was helping them actually achieve some degree of quan-
tifiable efficiency. Nationwide, observers believed the Clinton campaign
team did a much better job of political advertising.

Clinton's campaign created numerous issue ads to run at local television affiliates in swing states as early as the summer of 1995, or about
six months before the Republicans began advertising, and by January
1996 was running them daily. Dick Morris believed that early television
advertising was key to Clinton's victory. "There has never been anything
even remotely like it in the history of presidential elections. . . . We created the first fully advertised presidency in U.S. history."[11] Morris's penchant for self-aggrandizement aside, it is true that the Democrats used
advertising far more intelligently and aggressively than their opponents

did. So shrewd were they, in fact, in targeting specific media markets that their strategy passed just under the radar of most national journalists until well into the spring of 1996. "Thus, our best political reporters in print and television missed the top political story of 1995–1996," Morris wrote.[12] By contrast, Dole's advertising strategy seemed aimless. He flip-flopped over whether to use ads in Missouri, for example; first the polls indicated he ought not to bother, then they indicated he should. Even conservatives expressed envy for the opposition. As John Sununu grouchily declared late in the year, "The most effective thing the campaign for the Congress and the presidency have going for them on the Democratic side has been the ads—the Medi-scare ads by the union."[13]

Americans also believed, unfairly, that the president's commercials were the cleaner of the two. But political science professor Marion R. Just has since shown that that perception was not only untrue, but nearly the opposite of the truth: "Even though Dole used more positive spots than Clinton," that is, "the public judged Dole to be the more negative campaigner."[14] Yet the situation was actually far more distorted than even Professor Just outlined. She writes that "[a]s a whole, the 1996 campaign will go down as less negative than previous campaigns because both sides tended to focus on the records."[15] But other scholars have determined that 1996 campaign advertising was extraordinarily negative. Lynda Lee Kaid, for one, concludes that "1992 and 1996 were record-breaking years for negativity, especially for the Clinton campaigns. Clinton's percentage of negative attacks was the highest in history in his two general election campaigns."[16] Kaid also notes that the media branded Dole the more negative candidate, and the public believed so as well.

Negative news coverage of the president cropped up frequently. In June 1996, three of the Clintons' former Whitewater partners were indicted, an event which prompted an "avalanche of media coverage." Amid television specials on ABC and four-page exposés in the *Washington Post*, CNN talk show host Bernard Kalb wondered whether reporters were "putting the Clintons on trial."[17] The *Washington Post*'s Howard Kurtz complained that journalists had "gone too much into the speculation business," and the Public Broadcasting System's (PBS's) Ellen Hume agreed that to this point there was more conjecture than actual substance to the charges. The panelists, which also included veteran TV news correspondent Sander Vanocur, discussed the demands of a twenty-four-hour news cycle and the apparent lack of editing that went on. As was often the case during Clinton controversies, the press engaged in immediate hand-wringing and self-examination.

Summertime gave both parties a chance to capture favorable coverage, if not glowing headlines, with the onset of the conventions. And, predictably enough, both conventions basked in generally positive news. Of course, conventions over the last few decades have been so painstakingly controlled, there is little room for embarrassing episodes or unforeseeable conflicts. Some, in fact, have compared party conventions to political commercials and pageants.[18] Broadcast journalist Ted Koppel, among the critics of recent political conventions, left San Diego early because of what he thought was a lack of newsworthiness. The Republican convention was, indeed, a hyper-choreographed "media triumph" marked by carefully scripted organization and showy unity. Still, however self-conscious, it was nonetheless a public relations success. According to one scholar, the Republicans attracted as much attention from the television networks as the Democrats, and in the case of the vice presidential name on the ticket, twice as much.[19] The GOP received the expected boost in the polls following their convention, but a week and a half later, the Democratic Party got a lift of its own with its convention in Chicago.

The Democratic Party's convention was not quite as tranquil, however. Though the convention itself went smoothly and even grandly, external events conspired to crash the party. A tabloid newspaper issued a story saying that presidential adviser Dick Morris had been caught with a prostitute and that Morris had allowed her to listen in on conversations with his boss. The timing could not have been more embarrassing: Morris tendered his resignation the next day—the same day President Clinton was supposed to address the convention. As Elizabeth Arnold of National Public Radio summarized the situation, "Dick Morris . . . lost his job . . . after committing the worst sin of all in the business—he stepped on his own candidate's moment. In fact, he trampled all over it."[20] Morris's predicament could not help but bring more ridicule of the administration. Here was Clinton's chief strategist, brought in as a family-values guru because of the president's "extraordinary folly," committing some extraordinary folly of his own.[21] The "amoral man who tried to make the President look like a moral man has turned out to be an immoral man," Maureen Dowd wrote.[22]

The scandal did not end there, because Morris did not go quietly. First, he lambasted the media for its thirst for "sadistic yellow vitriol." Then he started complaining about White House leaks from his confidential personnel file and accused the Clinton administration of abusing its access to such documents. Still, the damage had been done through Morris's mere association with the president. Both men, said Dowd, "put polls above principles, winning above authenticity. . . . Mr. Morris said privately that Mr. Clinton was a hollow man. But maybe he meant it as a compliment."[23]

No other crises occurred for the rest of the campaign, and as autumn brought the debates there appeared only a slight increase in media interest. Clinton and Dole participated in two encounters, on October 6 and October 16, while their vice presidential partners met on October 9. The media showed up as usual, but the public seemed less interested than it had four years earlier. Ratings were down sharply—about 20 percent—from 1992.[24] Pundits no doubt contributed to the low ratings with their downplaying of the significance of the October face-offs. The candidates did, too, with their mainly nonconfrontational monologues. Observers noted more similarities than differences in their prepared comments, which could not have helped the challenger. "To the extent that Dole was unable to draw sharp distinctions between himself and Clinton, his candidacy was undermined."[25] CBS *Evening News* anchor Dan Rather even referred to the event as a "so-called debate." Howard Kurtz said on CNN's program, *Reliable Sources*, that when "there isn't any mud being thrown, you can almost sense the press was disappointed."[26] Kurtz's co-panelists on the program then debated whether moderator Jim Lehrer's questions had been tough enough. PBS's Ellen Hume said they had, but Dole had simply decided not to go on the attack, and her point appeared to settle the issue.

For many reporters, the real story about the debate was the warp-speed "spinning" that surrounded the event—the swarms of aides, agents, spokespersons, and assorted party flacks sent to talk to and guide journalists in their reporting. At the sight of such self-serving political flirtation, NBC correspondent John Rutherford quipped, "It reminds me of college rush week."[27] Before the debate even started, journalists received packets of information designed to challenge one candidate's facts and arguments. And during and after the debate, too, spinners handed out additional materials.

So, who won the debate? Such a question presupposes that debates are winnable, but in American presidential debates that is easily disputable. According to Martin Schram, debates "are not really about winning or losing; they're just about convincing voters to vote for Candidate X for president. That is all."[28] Schram points out that in 1992 most people thought Ross Perot had triumphed in the debate but nonetheless said they would vote for either Bush or Clinton. *Los Angeles Times* critic Howard Rosenberg wrote that the televised debates "are the ultimate fiction and the biggest redundancy of presidential campaigns. . . . [T]hey resolve nothing except which candidate gives the better performance in front of TV cameras on a given night."[29]

BIAS?

A popular bumper sticker appeared on cars and trucks during 1992. It read: "Annoy the Media; Vote for Bush." Was the sticker right that the media wanted Clinton to win? It certainly appeared that way to many Americans, and studies would eventually show that perception to be more than simply a hunch. In 1995, a survey reported that an overwhelming majority of journalists—approximately 90 percent—claimed to have voted for Bill Clinton in the '92 election. A year later, the Roper Center Review of Public Opinion and Polling publication, *The Public Perspective*, revealed that only 3 percent of journalists surveyed said they believed the Republicans' Contract with America was a serious reform proposal, while almost 60 percent called it merely an election-year ploy.[30] The bumper sticker of 1992 reappeared in 1996, this time urging people to annoy the media and vote for Dole. And toward the end of the campaign Bob Dole took up the cry himself. "We are not going to let the media steal this election," he said in late October. "The country belongs to the people, not the *New York Times*." Conservative writers like Cal Thomas shouted that Clinton had "the big media just where he wants them—as a wholly owned subsidiary of his re-election campaign."[31]

To what extent was Bob Dole's fortune in 1996 determined by an unfriendly media? As in 1992, most reporters indicated an affinity for the Democratic Party and for President Clinton. Yet, without question, Dole's own personal shortcomings played an important role. "Have you ever seen a worse-run presidential campaign than Bob Dole's?" CNN talk show host Bill Press bluntly asked a guest.[32] Michael Barone, the guest, a senior writer for *U.S. News and World Report* and the author of a recent essay on media bias, nearly acknowledged as much. Barone said that the Dole campaign did show signs of unravelling and was allowing its "internal fights" to get into the news. But Barone also made it clear that he believed America's media to be "monopartisan," "one-party":

Are these people all deliberately conspiring to produce unfair coverage and make everybody vote for their candidate? No, although you can find some examples of that. That's rare. . . . [B]ut on the other hand, is the product that they produce the same as if you had a 89 percent Bush-staffed media or a media that was like the voters were—43, 37, 19—in 1992? And the answer is of course not. The product is different in some ways. You look for the stories that you expect for your ideas of how the world works.[33]

Barone concluded by saying that the mainstream media in America were "reliably anti-Republican, but not reliably pro-Democratic." Former journalist and media critic Tom Rosenstiel agreed that there is liberal bias, but that it "comes out, not in secret support for Democratic candidates, but in inadequate coverage of conservative ideas. That's where Dole may have a legitimate point."[34] Other media watchers rightfully noted a tendency for journalists "occasionally [to] stop and ask whether they'd been too tough on the President, a question rarely—if ever—asked during a Republican presidency."[35]

Undisguised political favoritism was easily observable in 1996, too. One Washington correspondent attempting to question Mike McCurry about the president's fundraising practices was getting nowhere with the press secretary, when, to his surprise, he "found [him]self rebuked by colleagues." "Mike's a really nice guy," one journalist told him, by way of explanation.[36] And TV critic Tom Shales showed his true colors, perhaps, when he rendered this roseate glimpse of the presidential race:

It was, yes, a dull campaign, and kind of a sad one, with Dole seeming to get older and more desperate as it wore on. But it was not without its moments of excitement, and it was not without its passion. On Monday night, Bill Clinton gave what he called the last speech of the last campaign of his life, to enthusiastic supporters in Iowa. He was vibrant, he was eloquent, he was funny, he was charming, he was magnificent.[37]

A viewer watching the speech, Shales surmised, could hardly help but conclude that Clinton deserved reelection if only for his enthusiasm.

Not all journalists were so thoroughly charmed, though, and sometimes actual peeps of hostility toward the president could be heard. Believing his network had already switched to a commercial break on election night, veteran ABC journalist David Brinkley called President Clinton "a goddamn bore." "Out of respect and affection," one writer said, "ABC kept Brinkley up too late, and on the air one election too many."[38] Less than a week later, the seventy-six-year-old broadcaster personally apologized to the president in an interview on *This Week with David Brinkley*. Brinkley first congratulated Clinton on winning, then mentioned the embarrassing remark: "What I said . . . was both impolite and unfair. And I'm sorry. I regret it." "I accept that," the president responded. "I've said a lot of things myself late at night when I was tired, and you had really been through a rough day and I always believe you have to judge people on their whole work, and if you get judged based on your whole work, you come out way ahead." It was, coincidentally, Brinkley's last appearance on the show named for him. As one writer put it the next day, "Legendary television newsman David Brinkley went into semi-retirement yesterday with a bang and a whimper."[39]

In any case, there was less press about the campaign in 1996 than in previous years, and generally that trend favors the incumbent. It was as though American journalists had early on determined that Bob Dole couldn't beat Bill Clinton and therefore paid less attention to the contest. The 40 percent decline in both print and broadcast coverage certainly made it "harder for Dole to break through."[40] In addition, the press was also, according to *Forbes* media critic Terry Eastland, "enforcing a civility rule. . . . I don't think it wants Bob Dole to be negative."[41] And the compulsion toward the positive is a serious handicap for a challenger, who after all must criticize the incumbent in order to demonstrate why the electorate should make a change.

On his *Crossfire* program of October 25, Bill Press expressed his frustration at constantly hearing charges of media bias against Dole and for Clinton. Press pointed out a handful of critical books that had come out about the president, all of them ranging from the merely negative to the scandalous and outrageous. The titles included James Stewart's *Blood Sport*, Roger Morris's *Partners in Power*, R. Emmett Tyrrell's *Boy Clinton*, Gary Aldrich's *Unlimited Access*, and David Brock's *The Seduction of Hillary Clinton*. How can they say the president was getting "a free ride" in the media, Press wanted to know. "[I]t's like gang rape in the book world against the Clinton administration.[42] Press's guest on the program, Michael Barone of *U.S. News and World Report*, responded by saying that these literary indictments against the president were finding their way into book form because they were not finding access in newspapers and on television.

Yet, critical stories of the administration certainly surfaced in 1996, and particularly late in the year on the subject of campaign finance. The press, one editorial noted, had been "chock full of late-campaign disclosures about tainted money from Asian sources."[43] Allegations about Chinese American friends, Indonesian contributors, and Buddhist donors swirled around the White House in the fall of 1996. Hundreds of thousands of dollars were returned. According to some journalists, those reports cost Clinton at the voting booth, with "last-minute reactions to all the publicity about the President's unsavory fund raising" apparently moving additional Americans to cast their vote for Dole.[44] So the administration drew bad press, too, in 1996.

So, was media bias the reason Bob Dole lost in 1996? Hardly. The media did demonstrate a persistent prejudice against the Dole candidacy, but as Barone pointed out in the *Crossfire* program, media bias has generally had little to do with electoral outcomes:

[T]he bad news is that the media is monopartisan. The good news is people don't pay a lot of attention to us. Fifty years ago, the media was mostly Republican. Franklin Roosevelt, Harry Truman won five straight elections. Now the last 30 years the media has been mostly Democratic in the proportion of people that put it together, and the public has elected Republican presidents either five or six out of the last eight times.[45]

The real answer lies in the overall weakness of the Dole candidacy and the ineffectiveness of his campaign. One survey in the fall of 1995 revealed that voters' most common impression of Dole was that he was "old."[46] Indeed, 25 percent of Americans (and 37 percent of those over seventy!) indicated that they thought Dole was too old to run.[47] Polls also showed that Bob Dole was only able to mobilize three-quarters of registered Republicans, while the president was energizing over 90 percent of his base.[48] And, finally, every poll ever taken, including those taken as early as 1995, showed Dole unable to beat Clinton in either a two-way or a three-way race. Other Republicans polled better and likely would have done better. Indeed, one person consistently beat every candidate in the field: Colin Powell. Yet, Powell chose not to run. Had he done so, and as a Republican, surveys showed, he would have defeated Clinton easily.[49] Perhaps the most trenchant measure of Dole's weak candidacy was the extent to which the Clinton campaign embraced him as an opponent. In several of the Democrats' effective ads during 1995 and 1996, Gingrich was shown criticizing Medicare, but the Democrats reportedly held one showing Dole doing the same thing because they wanted to keep him viable to run against.[50]

As for Dole's campaign, even Republicans grumbled that he lacked a theme, a message, a cause. He seemed to be going through the motions without any degree of enthusiasm or even confidence. In an October chat with radio host Don Imus, Dole talked about the pros and cons of attacking Clinton as though he were thinking out loud: "We found in our surveys if you go on attack with Clinton—maybe it's the same if he attacks me, but we haven't seen it—that the first people who jump overboard are women." One reporter gasped at this confession, saying Dole had broken a "cardinal rule"—keeping one's survey research to oneself, a mistake Clinton never made.[51] Even at the end, on election night, Dole was forced to retract a premature concession note he had sent to the networks half an hour before polls closed in the West, "making this," one writer snorted, "the last flub in a flub-ridden campaign."[52] It was weaknesses like these, as much as anything the media did or did not do, which doomed the Republicans' quest for the White House in 1996. The American public showed far less interest that year than it had in 1992. Fewer people watched the debates in 1996, and fewer watched the returns on election night.[53]

THE NEW-MEDIA CIRCUIT

One of the distinctive characteristics of the 1992 campaign, perhaps the signature one, was the extent to which candidates aggressively pursued unconventional media strategies. There was a variety of innovations from that year: the use of toll-free telephone numbers, on-line services, satellite conferences, and, above all, the television talk show. Ross Perot had been the first to take advantage of such forums as *Larry King Live*, while Bill Clinton so mastered the talk show "visit" that he became what one might call "The Empathy Candidate," an archetypical virtuoso in the use of political-celebrity chat. Media strategist Mandy Grunwald had originated the idea so that Clinton could circumvent a hostile Washington press corps and still get his image, personality, and ideas across to the American people. And how did Clinton court such venues in the 1996 campaign? The answer is, he didn't have to. He had so early and so steadily maintained a comfortable lead in the polls, he did not believe frequent or regular talk show visits were necessary in 1996. Nor did Bob Dole, even though he badly needed to refashion his public image and recharge his favorability ratings, which mainly sagged during the campaign. The problem was that Dole seemed temperamentally unsuited for new-media forums. He was known for having a dry wit, yet he was neither bubbly nor telegenic, and hardly stirred pulses when he did appear on television programs.

Yet, talk shows were hardly irrelevant in 1996. In fact, by then, they were an established and acceptable tactic. The candidates' use of them was modest, however, compared with the phenomenon in 1992, mainly because in that year two exciting challengers with a fondness for the new forums milked them for all they were worth. The candidates did visit the talk shows in 1996; it was just that Bill Clinton did not need them as much, and Bob Dole did not receive as many invitations as he might have liked. Clearly, some of the novelty had worn off.

One interesting dimension in all of this is the Buchanan candidacy. Patrick Buchanan ran for and lost the Republican Party nomination in 1996. As in 1992, Buchanan did do well in a couple of primaries and attracted some fervent supporters but otherwise fizzled and dropped from the scene. The most interesting thing about his candidacy, however, was not its fringe constituency but the candidate's professional origins. Patrick Buchanan had never been a politician, a businessman, a military man, or a lawyer. His claim to fame was his role as a television pundit, an original host of the CNN talk show *Crossfire*. Though Clinton and Perot both famously used the talk show format with great success in 1992, media critic Howard Kurtz describes Buchanan as even more a media phenomenon: "Buchanan is a guy created by talk shows. [His] career the last two decades has essentially been slinging opinions."[54] Buchanan left the CNN program in February 1995, yet before doing so, he raised a placard on his final show with the following phone number printed on it, "1–800-GO-PAT-GO."

The talk show culture was here to stay, of course, and the melding of entertainment media and politics seemed permanent, too. But the so-called "new media" did not quite make the impact on the '96 campaign that they had appeared to in 1992. In fact, some observers wrote them off completely. Television critic Robert Bianco penned this bleak review: "If you're looking for media trends, the most interesting may be the death of the 'alternative media,' which had been hailed as the coming wave in 1992. This time around, there was no sax playing on late-night TV, no overhyped MTV forums, and little role for talk radio."[55] Of course, the apparent diminishment of these media might have had something to do with a retiring, unphotogenic seventy-three-year-old challenger, who was not determined to try anything to win.

In other areas, namely the Internet, the new media showed a significant rise in influence. At a time when only one in ten Americans subscribed to an on-line service, electronic electioneering had not yet entered its heyday, but according to the Media Studies Center, most of the candidates campaigning during the New Hampshire primary had their own websites. Republican primary candidate Phil Gramm's alone registered

197,425 "hits" during a five-month period and only cost $8,000. Gramm estimated that he reached perhaps seven to eight times as many people with this forum as he would have with the old method of a direct mailing.[56] So, the new media were not as conspicuous in 1996 as they had been four years earlier, but they were still important and even then still transforming the political process.

INTROSPECTION

Perhaps because of the press's boredom, the 1996 presidential campaign occasioned frequent discussions about the wider political process in the national media. Whether the issue was partisan bias, journalists' love for conflict, or the dominance of public opinion polls, newspaper columns and television programs were filled with contemplation, with philosophy. Writers and commentators wondered about their role, their impact, their performance. They questioned and criticized their relationship to political consultants and particularly to pollsters. "When poll after poll tells voters that Bob Dole is running far behind in the presidential race, do the surveys create a self-fulfilling reality?" asked the *New York Times*. The year's campaign, the *Times* writer said, "may be remembered as so infused by polls and survey research that President Clinton actually turned a standard polling question about whether the country is 'on the right track' into a campaign slogan."[57] Pollster Tom Smith elaborated: "Never have so many public polls measured the political election sentiments for so long. And never in the history of polling have voters been so sure of the outcome of an election."[58] Just a few weeks before, surveys had shown that nine out of ten Americans believed President Clinton would beat Bob Dole, and many observers sensed that the reason lay simply in the cumulative force of other polls—and in the way the mass media continually hyped them. "Who's ahead? is a perfectly valid question during a campaign," Max Frankel wrote, "but the pervasive polling has made it virtually the only subject of media concern."[59] Worse, while polls were still fraught with the usual margins of error, imprecision, and highly manipulable data, newsrooms were relying ever more heavily on the supposed significance of polls, but without sufficient respect for their inherent limitations.

Public opinion polling had, in fact, become so omnipresent and influential as almost to overshadow the role of journalists in the year's campaign. The press felt the slight and even tried to make a little noise of its own on election night with stagey, overproduced spectaculars. CBS anchor Dan Rather exhorted viewers to vote, "even told people out West it was crucial to vote to get your candidate the number he wanted, as if we vote to protect a point spread," one unamused critic wrote.[60]

But, of course, all the major news organizations had already gotten into the polling business themselves, not that you'd always know by what they said. "Journalists can be pretty snide about the tendency among politicians to dance with the polls, but news organizations often do the same," one writer admitted.[61] Since the 1984 and 1988 elections, everyone from *USA Today* to the *New York Times* to NBC to CNN has adopted nightly tracking polls, which are kept scrupulously updated and continually made prominent. Those defending polls' use say they are the best way to keep accurate track of the ongoing race, and therefore they are used a lot. Indeed, between September 3 and November 5, the Roper organization estimated, no fewer than 125 national polls would be administered.[62] "I think we have gone absolutely out of our minds about polls," says television journalist Jeff Greenfield.[63]

There were other concerns as well. Fred Exoo, a professor writing in the *Houston Chronicle*, organized most other complaints about the media into two categories: "News coverage of politics is cynical, and it's trivial." It is obsessed with insider tactics and, above all, with image. Reporters were too tempted not to guess what strategy political candidates and their campaign teams were cooking up, what they thought of certain public perceptions, and how they might react to the latest poll. As a result, Exoo says, reporters focus most of their energy on issues most Americans care little about. "This kind of reporting . . . reduces politics to a spectator sport and reduces reporters to the role of color commentators—'Ooh! He looked a little shaky on that dismount. That will cost him points with the judges.' "[64]

CONCLUSION

A weak challenger. A bored press. And with the conspicuous presence of ever-ubiquitous polls, it is no surprise that some journalists wrote off Bob Dole a little too quickly. Instead of the sixteen to eighteen-point lead most polls predicted throughout the year, President Clinton ended up winning by a margin of just eight percentage points. Most of the press believed Clinton would win all along, and most probably intended to vote for him. Summarizing journalists' feelings in the spring of 1996, Christopher Hanson described the mood of the press in a passage redolent of cynicism and arrogance:

In this campaign season's early phase the game was even more diverting than usual. We didn't just kill candidacies off. We resurrected them and killed them off again, as in playground wars of old. Each week, at times, every couple of days, our sand castle consensus was kicked down and eagerly rebuilt. But then, on or about March 12, far sooner than we had hoped, the dreaded specter was upon us: game over, drama dead, Bob Dole—Bob Dull, as the *Washington Post* called him in one headline—sews up nomination. Time to go home and eat all our broccoli.[65]

This passage contains, I think, the crux of the story of the 1996 campaign in the media: fundamental disinterest in the presidential race, a condescending incredulity over the Dole candidacy, and a degree of introspection bordering on self-absorption. Naturally, Hanson is trying to be funny as well, and his wit succeeds, but not before revealing what it is every political writer wants in a campaign—drama. It might be that a Dole campaign signified to the press a starchy return to old-media strategy, which was nothing if not boring and in Dole's case sure to be fatal. For all his legislative abilities, the Kansas congressman certainly did not loom then as a talk show dream-guest. Perhaps, ironically, the established media had come to depend on new-media politics, and the kind of candidate who could capitalize on it, for an entertaining political story no reporter could resist. From a journalistic perspective, at least, Bill Clinton in the White House guaranteed "interesting times."

NOTES

1. Dick Morris, *Behind the Oval Office: Winning the Presidency in the Nineties* (New York: Random House, 1997), p. 96.

2. Ibid., pp. 80–84.

3. Ibid., p. 37.

4. Many readers of *Behind the Oval Office*, including members of the Clinton administration, downplayed Morris's role. White House Press Secretary Mike McCurry said "some of it's wrong," while adviser George Stephanopoulos dismissed the memoir by calling it "a wholly accurate depiction of Dick's state of mind, and at times Dick was incredibly influential. . . . It's got too many holes to be history [however]. He confuses cause (Morris's advice) with effect (Clinton's actions)." Quoted in John F. Harris, "Morris's Tactics Still Hold Sway at White House," *Washington Post* (January 27, 1997), p. A1. Despite Morris's "self-obsessed portrait," Harris writes, "current and former Clinton aides, pressed on the inaccuraries, mostly point to small details. Independent reporting

of several of the important passages tend to buttress the consultant's account."
Ibid.

5. Christopher Hitchens, *No One Left to Lie to: The Triangulations of William Jefferson Clinton* (London: Verso, 1999), pp. 26–27.

6. Wilson Carey McWilliams, "The Meaning of the Election," in Gerald M. Pomper (ed.), *The Election of 1996: Reports and Interpretations* (Chatham, NJ: Chatham House, 1997), p. 241.

7. Media Studies Center/ADT Research study of the three television networks, cited in Marion R. Just, "Candidate Strategies and the Media Campaign," in Gerald M. Pomper (ed.), *The Election of 1996: Reports and Interpretations* (Chatham, NJ: Chatham House, 1997), p. 85.

8. Quoted on CNN, *Reliable Sources* (October 13, 1996).

9. Ibid.

10. Ibid.

11. Morris, *Behind the Oval Office*, pp. 138, 145.

12. Ibid., p. 140.

13. John Sununu, CNN, *Crossfire* (October 25, 1996).

14. Marion R. Just, "Candidate Strategies and the Media Campaign," p. 92.

15. Just, p. 93.

16. Lynda Lee Kaid, "Videostyle and the Effects of the 1996 Presidential Campaign Advertising," in Robert E. Denton, Jr., (ed.) *The 1996 Presidential Campaign: A Communication Perspective* (Westport, CT: Praeger Publishers, 1998), p. 156.

17. CNN, *Reliable Sources* (June 9, 1996).

18. David M. Timmerman and Gary M. Weier, "The 1996 Presidential Nominating Conventions: Good Television and Shallow Identification," in Robert E. Denton, Jr. (ed.), *The 1996 Presidential Campaign: A Communication Perspective* (Westport, CT: Praeger Publishers, 1998), p. 97.

19. Marion R. Just, "Candidate Strategies and the Media Campaign," in Gerald M. Pomper (ed.), *The Election of 1996: Reports and Interpretations* (Chatham, NJ: Chatham House, 1997), p. 87.

20. Elizabeth Arnold, National Public Radio, *Morning Edition* (August 30, 1996).

21. William Safire, "Morris vs. Clinton," *New York Times* (September 12, 1996), p. A23.

22. Maureen Dowd, "Liberties; Sadistic Yellow Vitriol," *New York Times* (September 1, 1996), IV, p. 9.

23. Ibid.

24. Marion R. Just, "Candidate Strategies and the Media Campaign," p. 87.

25. Robert V. Friedenberg, "The 1996 Presidential Debates," in Robert E. Denton, Jr. (ed.), *The 1996 Presidential Campaign: A Communications Perspective* (Westport, CT: Praeger Publishers, 1998), p. 119.

26. CNN, *Reliable Sources* (October 13, 1996).

27. Quoted in Eleanor Randolph and Elizabeth Shogren, "Before, During and After, Journalists Get Full Spin Cycle," *Los Angeles Times* (October 7, 1996), p. A12.

28. Martin Schram, "The Worst Debate Question: 'Who Won?' " *Cleveland Plain Dealer* (October 5, 1996), p. B10.

29. Howard Rosenberg, "Are Debates Necessary? That's, Well, Debatable," *Los Angeles Times* (October 4, 1996), p. F1.

30. *The Public Perspective* (October–November 1996).

31. Cal Thomas, "The Media Tilt," *New Orleans Times-Picayune* (October 28, 1996), p. B5.

32. CNN, *Crossfire* (October 25, 1996).

33. Michael Barone, CNN, *Crossfire* (October 25, 1996).

34. Quoted in Howard Kurtz, "Dole Attack Rings True with Some in Press; But Others Say Nominee's Charges of 'Liberal Bias' Are Not Reflected in Recent Coverage," *Washington Post* (October 27, 1996), p. A22.

35. Tim Graham, *Pattern of Deception: The Media's Role in the Clinton Presidency* (Alexandria, VA: Media Research Center, 1996), p. 115.

36. Douglas Turner, "Good Spin Deserves Another as Clinton's Media Massage Passes from Expert to Master," *Buffalo News* (September 27, 1999), p. B2.

37. Tom Shales, "The Bill Clinton Show, Renewed Till the 21st Century," *Washington Post* (November 6, 1996), p. F1.

38. Robert Bianco, "Network Exit Poll Debate Is Raging Once More," *Pittsburgh Post-Gazette* (November 7, 1996), p. A17.

39. Bill Thomas, "Not Quite Goodnight," *Baltimore Sun* (November 11, 1996), p. D1.

40. Howard Kurtz, "Dole Attack Rings True with Some in Press; But Others Say Nominee's Charges of 'Liberal Bias' Are Not Reflected in Recent Coverage," *Washington Post* (October 27, 1996), p. A22.

41. CNN, *Reliable Sources* (October 13, 1996).

42. CNN, *Crossfire* (October 25, 1996).

43. Editorial, "Thickening Tale of Tainted Money," *Baltimore Sun* (December 18, 1996), p. A22.

44. Max Frankel, "Margins of Error," *New York Times* (December 15, 1996), VI, p. 34.

45. CNN, *Crossfire* (October 25, 1996).

46. Linda Fowler and Tami Buhr, WMUR-Dartmouth Poll, October 1–4, 1995, cited in Marion R. Just, "Candidate Strategies and the Media Campaign," p. 80.

47. David W. Moore, "Age Issue Hurts Dole in Presidential Race," *Gallup Poll Monthly* 366 (March 1996), p. 32.

48. Lydia Saad and Frank Newport, "Dole Not Maximizing Support from Republican Voters," *Gallup Poll Monthly* 349 (June 1996), p. 10.

49. Lydia Saad, "Powell's Best Bet: Run as a Republican," *Gallup Poll*

Monthly 361 (October 1995), p. 12. And Clinton repeatedly told Dick Morris that he believed Powell could beat him. Morris, *Inside the Oval Office*, p. 155.

50. Morris, *Inside the Oval Office*, p. 184.

51. Alison Mitchell, "In an Era When the Polls Are King, Cookie-Cutter Campaigns," *New York Times* (November 4, 1996), p. B8.

52. Robert Bianco, "Network Exit Poll Debate Is Raging Once More," *Pittsburgh Post-Gazette* (November 7, 1996), p. A17.

53. ABC, CBS, and NBC posted ratings of 28.5, a 42 percent share, in 1996, while in 1992 they recorded a 39.1 rating and 57 percent share. Cited in ibid.

54. Kurtz, quoted in Drew Jubera, "Campaign '96: The Candidate Talk Show Built," *Atlanta Constitution* (February 24, 1996), p. A10.

55. Robert Bianco, "Network Exit Poll Debate Is Raging Once More," *Pittsburgh Post-Gazette* (November 7, 1996), p. A17.

56. Media Study Center, *Media & Campaign '96 Briefing*, no. 1 (New York: The Freedom Forum, April 1996), p. 9.

57. Alison Mitchell, "In an Era When Polls Are King, Cookie-Cutter Campaigns," *New York Times* (November 4, 1996), p. B8.

58. Tom W. Smith, quoted in Bill Lambrecht, "Polls Can Drive Campaign Tactics, Voter Perceptions," *St. Louis Post-Dispatch* (October 27, 1996), p. A7.

59. Max Frankel, "Margins of Error," *New York Times* (December 15, 1996), VI, p. 34.

60. Robert Bianco, "Network Exit Poll Debate Is Raging Once More," *Pittsburgh Post-Gazette* (November 7, 1996), p. A17.

61. James Bennet, "Use of Daily Election Polls Generates Debate in Press," *New York Times* (October 4, 1996), p. A24.

62. Bill Lambrecht, "Polls Can Drive Campaign Tactics, Voter Perceptions," *St. Louis Post-Dispatch* (October 27, 1996), p. A7.

63. Quoted in James Bennet, "Use of Daily Election Polls Generates Debate in Press," *New York Times* (October 4, 1996), p. A24.

64. Fred Exoo, "Election Season Brings a Battle for Media's Soul," *Houston Chronicle* (September 30, 1996), p. A19.

65. Christopher Hanson, "Lost in Never-Never-Land," *Columbia Journalism Review* (May/June 1996), p. 41.

5

The Road to Impeachment

INTRODUCTION

Only a year after beginning his second term in office, Bill Clinton was in trouble again—in fact, the most serious trouble of his presidency. "If there's one thing we've learned about . . . Clinton," a journalist said, "it's that just as he gets through with one scrape, another one's right around the corner."[1] Unfortunately for America's 42nd president, his worst personal traits coincided with a profound cultural shift in the American media.

In the 1990s, print and broadcast journalism alike were becoming more prone to covering celebrity scandals. Cover stories in *Time* and *Newsweek*, for example, increasingly resembled those in *People* magazine.[2] And network news divisions sometimes appeared indistinguishable from their entertainment departments. According to a study sponsored by the Project for Excellence in Journalism, one of every seven network news stories in 1997 (a year *before* the Lewinsky affair) involved a scandal, while in 1977 only one in two hundred stories did.[3] Local television affiliates were often worse, running marqueed segments of an actor's comments about national politics, a movie star's tape-recorded 911 call as top-story news, or allowing "trash-tv" hosts on as political commentators.[4] Clearly, something had changed.

A hundred years after its most famous emergence, sensationalism had once again returned full-force to American culture, permeated the media, and established itself even among the intelligentsia. The "yellow press," in a sense, was back. Only now its practitioners were represented by more than just a couple of dozen guys with printing presses; they were everywhere, in mindboggling new venues, and they fed on scandals. Small wonder, then, that so many politicians—by one count, three of the last five presidents and two of the last three speakers of the house[5]— have undergone such ordeals. Scandals, in short, "have become the dominant feature of tabloid journalism . . . [and] have vaulted tabloid values to the forefront of mainstream news practice."[6] With the proliferation of video "news magazines," entertainment programs, and cable talk shows, television, in particular, was undergoing an unprecedented obsession with sensational controversies and speculative chat. The double-murder trial of O. J. Simpson in 1995, in fact, had singlehandedly launched the success of cable newcomers like Court TV and MSNBC, and solidified the reputation of channels like CNBC, television networks devoted to gabby "infotainment." "Because talk is cheap—economically and otherwise—you can watch talk shows 24 hours a day," a Canadian journalist observed from across the border. "As such, American discourse is framed and defined by talk shows."[7] So there was an unquestionable market for graphic exposés and loud confrontations. Then, in the heyday of a culture characterized by *Jerry Springer*, a scandal-prone media and a scandal-prone president crossed paths. What was the result? The blending of news and entertainment that had provided lifesaving forums for Bill Clinton's spectacular campaign in 1992 was also doing daily damage to the image and legitimacy of his presidency in 1998.

In this chapter, I will briefly discuss some of the earlier scandals, before turning to the uproar that almost removed a president from office. It should be emphasized that Bill Clinton was no mere victim in all this. Indeed, I think in many ways he bears much of the responsibility. But a particular media context at a particular time in American history put the president in a bizarre predicament: In an "all-entertainment-all-the-time" climate, his foibles became constant fodder, but by the same token it was difficult for the public to take them completely seriously, except to disapprove in a vague sort of way. Impeach a crook, yes, but what do you do about a laughingstock?

SCANDAL REVIEW

Personal scandal always accompanied Bill Clinton's political career, at least on the national scene. From the moment he declared his intention to run for the presidency in 1991 through his departure from office in 2001, there has never been a time without allegations, inquiries, investigations, lawsuits, or trials. Few pundits, other than conservative ones, failed to cite the fierce and aggressive political opposition Clinton inspired as one of the causes. All presidents have had to endure irrepressible partisan foes, but there was something different with Bill Clinton. And from time to time journalists wrestled with the proper description of that intangible something. Whether writers chalked up Clinton's frequent crises to moral vacancy, to recklessness, or to a certain inexplicable self-destructiveness,[8] most observers nonetheless recognized Clinton's penchant for frequently winding up in trouble.

Of course, Clinton's quest for the presidency in 1992 was itself born of scandal. In that year, he faced one firestorm after another—first, regarding his use of marijuana while a young man; second, involving a long-term extramarital affair with Gennifer Flowers; and third, a flap over the circumstances surrounding his avoidance of military service during the Vietnam War. With all these issues, Bill Clinton demonstrated a pattern of compounding questionable behavior with unconvincing dissimulation. Had he smoked marijuana? He said he had, but never inhaled. Had he been drafted for duty during the Vietnam War? He said he never got an induction notice. Didn't he receive a waiver from service? He admitted he had, but never mentioned reneging on his promise to join the University of Arkansas ROTC and going back to England instead.

And then there was Gennifer Flowers. No, he insisted, he had not had an affair with Flowers; she had only changed her story because a tabloid rag was willing to pay her a lot of money for a lurid tale. When Flowers held a press conference soon afterward and played recorded phone conversations between herself and the governor, everyone knew Bill Clinton was lying. Desperate to salvage his reputation, the candidate went on the CBS television program *60 Minutes* to present, along with his wife, their side of the story. Holding Hillary's hand, Clinton admitted "having caused pain in his marriage," but said he was trying to repair the damage and move on. The appearance helped him in his campaign but never quite restored his personal credibility.

Clinton's troubled past continued to haunt him in the White House. In January 1994, Attorney General Janet Reno named Robert Fiske as independent counsel to look into the Whitewater land deal, which the Clintons had invested in while in Arkansas. Allegations circulated that then-governor Clinton had used improper influence in halting an investigation of one of his Whitewater partners, James McDougal, whose Madison Guaranty Savings and Loan bank had folded and was under review. Fiske determined, however, that no evidence existed to corroborate the charges against Clinton, and in June he cleared the president. The House and Senate banking committees had other ideas, though, and reopened the investigation. A new independent counsel then took Fiske's place, forty-eight-year-old Kenneth Starr. One year later, in June 1995, Webster Hubbell, Clinton's former associate attorney general, was sentenced to prison for tax evasion and mail fraud. Former Arkansas governor Jim Guy Tucker had already been indicted, though on charges unrelated to Whitewater. And three months later, James and Susan McDougal were indicted for providing fraudulent loans. While these associations, as well as the Clintons' own murky involvement in Whitewater, damaged the president's reputation, the investigations never seemed to hurt him directly. And when journalists took him, or his wife, on too directly, as William Safire did in the winter of 1996, the president's ratings climbed while the press drew boos.

Clinton's predilection for extramarital affairs turned out to be his Achilles' heel, however. "Bimbo eruptions," a recurring description of the Arkansas governor's most prominent vulnerability in the '92 campaign, also plagued Bill Clinton during his two terms in the White House. On May 6, 1994, a former Arkansas state employee, Paula Corbin Jones, filed a lawsuit alleging that when Clinton was governor he had sexually harassed her in a hotel room. Later that year, a federal judge ruled that the lawsuit would have to wait until Clinton left office, because as president he deserved an immunity from distracting personal litigation. In January 1996, however, two out of three judges serving on the 8th Circuit Court of Appeals in St. Louis declared that ruling invalid. The president's lawyers complained that such lawsuits could effectively stymie an administration, and they filed a brief with the U.S. Supreme Court, which agreed in June to look at their case. Seven months later, the high Court did. But by a unanimous vote, it allowed the suit to go forward.

At that point, the press began to take the story more seriously. Articles on the subject cropped up with increasing frequency throughout 1997, and television programs became more likely to play up the issue. Until then, though, the lawsuit got little attention. Nor were journalists exactly polarized by the story. Since the lawsuit was first filed, many writers doubted Clinton but thought little of Paula Jones, whom *The Nation* once described as "more like Tonya Harding than Anita Hill."[9] What the Paula Jones lawsuit did was polarize liberals, some of whom rejected her claims out of hand because she received funds from anti-Clinton conservatives, while others grudgingly requested that Jones be allowed to prove her case in court. Of the former, feminist and law professor Susan Estrich wrote in *USA Today* that she thought Jones was lying and persecuting the president.[10] Of the latter, Katha Pollitt, an associate editor for *The Nation*, questioned feminists' commitment to their own principles for attacking the president's accuser. Pollitt singled out Susan Estrich's column in *USA Today*, which suggested that Jones and her defenders had forgotten all about individual responsibility—"as if feminists by the millions were following Jones on a take-back-the-night parade past the White House instead of holding their breath and hoping she dies."[11]

For more than two years after Jones first filed the lawsuit, most major news organizations shied away from the story. Through 1996 Stuart Taylor was one of the few journalists of national stature to draw attention to the case. He accused American elites of writing Jones off for superficial reasons. "Indeed, many people—especially lawyers and others of the intellectual and monied classes—need only see a newspaper photograph of Jones, with her big hair and overdone makeup, to discount her claims."[12] Taylor's piece in a minor publication did prompt larger fry to reconsider, however. A writer for the *San Francisco Chronicle*, for example, confessed that she, too, must "plead guilty to snobbery."[13]

With the 1997 ruling, Jones's case began to move forward and the press started to take a closer look. *Newsweek* was the first with a detailed examination of the lawsuit and an assessment of what it might mean to the Clinton presidency. At the time, the writers were simply analyzing the case in the context of explosive gender battles like the Clarence Thomas/Anita Hill face-off, a he-said, she-said dispute about sexual harassment. In retrospect, the article seems stunningly prophetic:

When Bill Clinton contemplates the scandals that could ruin his second term, what worries him most is not the vast machinery of the special prosecutor investigating Whitewater or the potential for endless congressional hearings over shady contributions to his presidential campaign. His real concern, say his friends, is the sexual harassment suit filed against him by Paula Jones. Legally, most experts agree, the case has some holes. But it still has the potential to make Clinton's life hellish in the months and years ahead.[14]

Through Jones's lawyers, *Newsweek* reporter Michael Isikoff was able to track down Kathleen Willey, a woman who claimed that the president made an improper advance toward her inside the Oval Office. Through Willey, Isikoff met former White House employee Linda Tripp and publicist Lucianne Goldberg, two women eager to collude on a profitable book baring personal presidential secrets. It was an odd association— these three people: Isikoff wanted from Tripp information with a relevant connection to the Jones lawsuit; Tripp and Goldberg wanted an article from Isikoff that would introduce Tripp to the book-buying public. Then, in the fall of 1997, someone (probably Linda Tripp) made anonymous phone calls to Paula Jones's lawyers suggesting they subpoena Tripp and White House intern Monica Lewinsky. When those subpoenas materialized, Isikoff finally had his connection, and Tripp and Goldberg finally got their article. And so, two book-deal conspirators, anxious to capitalize on political celebrity, however notorious, were largely responsible for making an intern's affair with the president public knowledge and rendering Monica Lewinsky a household name.

Yet, it wasn't *Newsweek* that first broke the news to the American people. The magazine's editors had decided to wait a few days for additional information. Befitting the new-media environment of the 1990s, the scoop came from a little-known Internet outlet devoted to celebrity news and political gossip, a website created by Matt Drudge. Drudge had spoken with Goldberg on the evening of Saturday, January 17, 1998, and was filled in on the Lewinsky affair and the pending *Newsweek* piece. Several hours later, at about one in the morning, Drudge mentioned both the intern and the skewered magazine story. Later that day, the Drudge rumor briefly made its way onto the Sunday news talk show, ABC's *This Week*, before cohost Sam Donaldson counselled caution. For the next couple of days, a handful of news organizations—principally ABC, *Newsweek*, and the *Washington Post*, but also the *Los Angeles Times* and the *New York Times*—worked feverishly to follow up sources and nail down leads. By Wednesday, January 21, the stories came tumbling out from these organizations' pages and programs, as well as their own official website updates. Cable programs had a feast. Media critic Steven Brill described CNBC's saturation coverage: "MSNBC's sister cable-TV channel is talking about the intern allegations almost nonstop. For the next 100 days, the fledgling cable channel would become virtually all Monica, all the time."[15]

Paula Jones's lawsuit was the seed from which came the disclosure about Kathleen Willey, the news about Monica Lewinsky, and finally, of course, the president's eventual impeachment by the House of Representatives. Yet, if David nearly slew Goliath in all this, David had some help: two determined groupies and the talk-crazy media.

The extent to which Ken Starr deserves blame usually depends on who is making the evaluation. Democrats have gone to great lengths to villainize him, while Republicans generally paint him as a sainted martyr. But both groups now appear to recognize the inherent evils of the Independent Counsel Act and to agree that without substantial reform its dangers probably outweigh its benefits. In 1998, nonetheless, Starr was probably the most hated man in America. Websites lampooning him sprang up in cyberspace. He became the butt of nearly as many jokes on late-night television as did the president. And his investigation even inspired the birth of a new magazine, *Brill's Content*. Media entrepreneur Steven Brill printed the first issue that summer, along with an exhaustive cover story that diligently strove to take the independent counsel's credibility apart piece by piece. Brill does concede in this meticulous, thirty-page analysis that Ken Starr would never have gotten anywhere without the initial conspiracy to squeeze out a scandal or without the "infotainment" delirium that pumped the story: The "competition for scoops to toss out into a frenzied, high-tech news cycle seems to have so bewitched almost everyone that the press eagerly let the man in power write the story—once Linda Tripp and Lucianne Goldberg put it together for him."[16] Brill's account is a fascinating and indispensable one, maybe the best available on the origins of the story. Still, his premise—right-wing conspiracy and journalistic stupidity—falls short of completely explaining why the scandal arose and broke as it did. In his passion to condemn the press, Brill seems to overlook the extent to which many established media organizations, print journalism in particular, bent over backward to avoid hyping the story. Former newsman Michael Gartner talked to newspaper managers, in fact, who described a powerful reluctance: "Alan Murray, Washington bureau chief of the *Wall Street Journal*, said it was a 'race to be last' in printing sex news about the president. A *New York Times* editor told his staff, 'This is the only area of news where I can't imagine wanting to be first. I need not just an excuse to do it. I need to be deprived of my last excuse not to do it.' "[17] There are thus three missing pieces in Brill's analysis, I would argue. One is something he touches on but slights as a central factor: the thirst in political entertainment for personal scandal. Even Tripp and Goldberg, Brill's primary villains, can be seen as mere participants in this culture of exposé, as exhibitionists eager to cash in on the same commodity peddled by CNBC, Drudge, and the *Washington Post*. Another element was simply Bill Clinton's folly. A presidential affair in the midst of a scandal-crazy society was risky. But flirting with perjury was absolutely reckless. Finally, Brill altogether misses what might indeed be the most significant factor of all: Clinton's method of damage control. Former *Wall Street Journal* reporter James Stewart describes it as "drop-by-drop concessions." All during the Whitewater investigation, he says, the administration responded to the scandal by choosing to "brush it aside, promise full support, then frustrate every inquiry."[18] However much time in the short run this tactic would buy, in the long run it was sure to aggravate and challenge journalists, not placate or deter them. Bob Woodward, assistant managing editor of the *Washington Post* and one of the journalists who exposed Richard Nixon's wrongdoings, agreed that President Clinton demonstrated a consistent paranoia about the press: "During the pre-Lewinsky phase of the Whitewater investigation, from 1994 to early 1995, the Clintons and their attorney David Kendall reacted too many times as if the scandal were Watergate. They seemed to be hiding."[19] The excruciatingly slow way in which the president often tried to extricate himself from embarrassing predicaments may not only explain the particular momentum of the Lewinsky story but also the president's general reputation as a scandal-prone politician. It might not be the case, then, that he was always stumbling into a lot of new scandals, but, rather, because of his tactics, that he was just never fully able to escape from the few he was in. When faced with controversy or criticism, that is, Bill Clinton often took senseless risks that made matters worse.

MONICA

She was a plump and pretty intern working in the White House. Until 1998, her name was unknown to the general public. Then, on January 21, three newspaper stories appeared about her, followed by more than 1,600 during the next ten days.[20] In short order, Monica Lewinsky became a political embarrassment, a national joke, and even something of a cultural icon. Lewinsky was a White House intern in the mid-1990s who had gotten to know the president, flirted, and eventually become intimate with him. Her access to the White House was cut short by a change of duties—like Tripp, Lewinsky was transferred to the Pentagon—but apparently she harbored Clinton no ill will. She had tried to regain employment closer to the Oval Office. And although among friends she sometimes referred to the president as "The Big Creep" and "Butthead," Lewinsky plainly never intended to go public with news of her affair, nor did she seem unconcerned about Clinton's reputation and privacy. She even risked perjury charges in early January when she swore in an affidavit that the two had never had a sexual relationship. Not by choice, then, did she become a witness for the prosecution.

The substance of Lewinsky's original affidavit was the president's story as well. In a six-hour deposition made on January 17, Clinton denied sexual relations with the former intern, though his line throughout much of 1998 simply claimed that there had been no improper relationship, and that Jones's lawyers and Independent Counsel Kenneth Starr were desperate to pin something on him. Clinton decided to try to douse the scandal's flames with a public statement. On January 26, after answering questions during a public appearance, he told reporters he had something else to say. Looking directly into the camera, the president spoke in a firm, angry tone: "I want to say something to the American people. I want you to listen. . . . I did not have sexual relations with that woman, Miss Lewinsky. I never told anybody to lie—not a single time, never. These allegations are false, and I need to go back to work for the American people." The president also encouraged his staff, his cabinet, and even various Democrats around the country to stress both points, and they obliged. On the NBC program *Meet the Press*, Clintonite journalist Gene Lyons of the *Arkansas Democrat-Gazette* said he wouldn't be surprised if Clinton did have a sexual encounter, but that such an encounter wouldn't necessarily mean he had been at fault:

If you take someone like the President, who a lot of women would find attractive if he came to fix their garbage disposal, and you make him the President of the United States, the alpha male of the United States of America, and you sexualize his image with a lot of smears and false accusations so that people think he's Tom Jones or Rod Stewart, then a certain irreducible number of women are going to act batty around him.[21]

Even Hillary Clinton pitched in to defend her husband. She appeared on NBC's morning program, *Today*, to offer some "spin" of her own: "The great story here for anybody willing to find it and write about it and explain it is this vast right-wing conspiracy."

In the meantime, the president did his best to pretend the scandal was not affecting White House business. Aides arranged as many photo opportunities showing Clinton busy with work as they could. And the State of the Union address, delivered on January 27, 1998, contained no mention whatsoever of the controversy. When aides tipped off the press a few days before the speech that the president's remarks would make no reference to Lewinsky, journalists were baffled. Wasn't there "something surreal about it?" ABC's Sam Donaldson wanted to know.[22] How could the president not address the turmoil in his biggest official address of the year?

Howard Kurtz, the *Washington Post* media critic, vividly captured the exasperation of journalists like Donaldson, who were confused and somewhat unnerved by President Clinton's teflon-coated good luck in the winter of 1998:

[The Washington press corps] has been supremely frustrated for the past year as Clinton kept slip-sliding his way through the scandalous muck. The president had maintained his extraordinary popularity despite their dogged efforts to hold him accountable for what they saw as the misconduct and the evasions that marked his administration. He had connected with the American public, and they had largely failed. Clinton, in their view, had gotten away with it. Until now.[23]

Kurtz described the half-hour bombardment of questions, some 150, launched at Clinton's press secretary, Mike McCurry, on that initial, January 21, 1998, briefing about the scandal. Poised by television cameras, some of them—like CNN, Fox News, and MSNBC—broadcasting live, reporters tensely waited. When McCurry emerged, they grilled him about the precise meaning of words in the president's statement that there had been no improper relationship between him and Lewinsky. What kind of relationship was it? Could he define "improper"? "I'm not going to parse the statement," McCurry declared, hoping to terminate the inquiry. But the correspondents were not so easily discouraged. They kept at it: Why hadn't the administration used the word "sexual" instead of "improper"? What kind of relationship would the president say it had been?

Naturally, McCurry did his best to avoid questions about Lewinsky, by referring reporters to specially designated spokespersons who played the role of "bad cop."[24] Usually, his deputy, Joe Lockhart, or one of the White House's personal stock of attorneys handled such inquiries. But McCurry was nonetheless often compelled to address certain aspects of the scandal and specific questions. With the Lewinsky scandal, his "strategy of saving himself" ultimately "broke down."[25] The normally unflappable press secretary could not keep his guard up indefinitely. On February 16, he admitted to Roger Simon of the *Chicago Tribune* that an "innocent explanation" was probably unlikely as that would have already come out. By implying that there *was* something unseemly about the Clinton-Lewinsky relationship, McCurry appeared either to be adding his own doubts that the president was telling the truth, or preparing the press for a kind of concession from Clinton himself. Either way, that was not the strategy or the response the White House had in mind, and McCurry quickly corrected himself, and harshly, in subsequent conversations. He described his comments in the *Tribune* as "a lapse in sanity," said that he'd shown that "only a fool answers hypothetical questions," and insisted that he had put himself "in the doghouse."[26]

Some in the press expressed sympathy: "Possibly, McCurry is fed up with enduring the daily indignity of responding to reporters' questions with evasions and half-truths," remarked one.[27] Many more journalists, though, were becoming impatient with the administration and its chief spokesman, the *New York Times*, for example, calling the press secretary's recent self-censure "goofy" and dubbing his pattern of persistent noncooperation "The McCurry Doctrine." The same *Times* editorial summarized the effect of such policy: "Briefing-room credibility has decayed further with the imposition of a dead zone around the Lewinsky case."[28] McCurry was by then making quite clear that not only had he not discussed the details of the Monica Lewinsky story with the president (in order to protect Clinton's attorney-client privilege), but that he did not *want* to know any of the details. "We still pounded him with Lewinsky questions," UPI correspondent Helen Thomas said. "But in order for him to stay focused, he had to distance himself. . . . [I]t was a survival technique."[29] Legal survival, too: McCurry did not want to subject himself to a subpoena from Ken Starr by getting in the midst of strategy talks about Monica. Not everyone was as charitable as Helen Thomas, however. Another *New York Times* editorial noted McCurry's popularity among journalists, but said his determination not to be informed about the Lewinsky controversy set a bad example for other public servants.[30] Most journalists, though, pitied the likable press secretary's difficult position and generally showed more patience with him one-on-one.

By March, the scandal deepened when new allegations suddenly came forward. The CBS program *60 Minutes* aired an interview on March 15 by correspondent Ed Bradley. The segment introduced viewers to Kathleen Willey, a Democratic volunteer who claimed the president had made an improper advance toward her while she was inside the Oval Office talking to Clinton about securing a job with the administration. Willey's interview "shook the White House like an earthquake," one writer remarked.[31] In the next few weeks, however, parts of Willey's story seemed to crumble a little. The White House released friendly letters

Willey had written to Clinton over the years since the alleged incident took place. And when it turned out that Willey's lawyer, Daniel Gecker, had all along been fishing around for a book deal with Hollywood publishers and tabloid papers before opting for *60 Minutes*, this portion of Scandal '98 appeared to be fizzling rapidly.

The pervasive nature of such thunderbolt journalism worried politicians and journalists alike—the latter, at least, when they had time to catch their breath. A special round table discussion on *Larry King Live* in March featured six former press secretaries, who talked about the crisis facing the president, Mike McCurry's performance in dealing with it, and the current state of the news business in America. Reagan secretary Larry Speakes described the tough spot Clinton's press secretary was in: "Mike McCurry is damned if he does, and damned if he doesn't. He tries to go for the facts, and the boss gets mad at him. He tries not to have the facts, and the press gets mad at him."[32] George Christian, press secretary to Lyndon B. Johnson, noted that McCurry seemed to have "raised stonewalling to a new level," then explained that it might be the result of a White House overrun with and apparently "run by" lawyers, a situation that did not exist three decades earlier. All agreed with Carter secretary Jody Powell that the political process had "become much nastier, much more personal, much more partisan" than before. And, finally, the former press secretaries criticized the media for their gusto for gossip, Larry Speakes, in particular, describing American journalism as "a rumor mill run wild."

But the "rumor mill" had apparently not yet scandalized the American people. At a time when most people said they thought Clinton was lying, the scandal did not otherwise appear to be hurting the president's overall standing with the public. Although many Americans expressed displeasure with his personal behavior, they overwhelmingly approved of the job he was doing, liked the direction the country was moving in as well as its unprecedented prosperity, and, finally, concluded that the president should continue in office. Polls indicated that Americans were quickly tiring of the scandal, and that they believed the charges against Clinton but nevertheless thought, 'so what?'—a trend that continued with almost eerie stability: "With each new revelation, Americans became more convinced of Clinton's guilt but less supportive of his removal from office."[33] A Gallup survey during the spring showed that 63 percent of people polled actually wanted the Jones case thrown out.[34]

Gallup's canvassers had already detected an "apparent backlash" against the way the media had handled the scandal. Three out of four

Americans said there was too much coverage, one out of two said the media were acting "irresponsibly," and one in three even believed the media were enjoying Clinton's predicament.[35] Clearly, this was not a good public review of the Fourth Estate. "In the sex scandal story that has cast a cloud over the presidency, Bill Clinton does not stand to be the only loser," veteran journalist Jules Witcover wrote. "No matter how it turns out, another will be the American news media, whose reputation as a truth-teller to the country has been besmirched by perceptions, in and out of the news business . . . about how the story has been re-ported."[36]

Perhaps as a result of this "bad press" for the press, many in the media displayed a sort of grumpy weariness, and midway through the year there appeared to be a "relative lull" in national interest in the scandal.[37] In April, a federal judge had thrown out Paula Jones's lawsuit, and now the White House seemed to allow itself the luxury of relaxing a little bit after months of fear and tension. Journalists were no less agitated or aggressive at press conferences, but the whole story had hardened into a sort of brutal and predictable "ritual," one writer observed.[38] Things had momentarily stabilized, even if they remained unpleasant. Reporters in the West Wing still jousted regularly with McCurry about what exactly the president had done with Lewinsky, what exactly he had said to her, and what exactly he was feeling and thinking now. They wrestled se-mantically with every statement McCurry made on the subject, groped for inferences and potential syllogisms. After pushing the press secretary to exhaustive lengths one day about what he himself knew but hadn't yet said, McCurry snapped at the journalists there for their freewheeling speculations, and singled out ABC correspondent Sam Donaldson in par-ticular: "Sam, what is widely reported and what is the truth may or may not be the same thing. I mean, you don't know what she has said, and none of us do, and I know you all are going to have to run out and yak and yak and yak forever about this, but it's going to be based on very few facts."[39]

"At a time when the media and presidency once again seem bitter enemies," when combative sessions such as these became the rule and not the exception, McCurry was fully and daily under more intense strain than the man he represented.[40] In July, it was announced that, following Congress's recess in the fall, Deputy Press Secretary Joe Lockhart would succeed his boss as chief spokesperson for the president. Lockhart had earned a reputation as an aggressive partisan with a wicked sense of humor, someone who was less polished but much fiercer than McCurry.

Clinton made an appearance at the daily briefing to announce the news himself and to toast his outgoing press secretary: "Mike McCurry has set the standard by which future White House press secretaries will be judged," the president declared. "In an age where Washington has come to be governed by a 24-hour news cycle and endless cable channels with their special niche audiences, Mike has redefined the job of press secretary in a new and more challenging era."[41] Many in the media were equally commendatory. A *Washington Post* writer, for example, noted that McCurry had "helped steer President Clinton through three years of often hostile media fire,"[42] while the *Los Angeles Times* remarked that McCurry had actually "helped keep the Clinton presidency afloat through its rockiest days."[43]

Little did the *Los Angeles Times* know that things would get considerably worse. After cutting an immunity deal with prosecutors at the end of July, Monica Lewinsky agreed to testify for the independent counsel that she did have a sexual relationship with the president, and on August 7, she delivered her testimony. Within two weeks, Bill Clinton was ready to change his story, too. On August 17, the same day as his grand jury appearance, President Clinton went on national television to admit that he had engaged in inappropriate conduct with Lewinsky, that he was sorry, and regretted it. The confession was devastating, both for the administration and for the Democratic Party, many of whose members had passionately defended the president and strongly attacked the independent counsel. California senator Dianne Feinstein said her "trust in his credibility has been badly shattered."[44] It was also an unprecedented embarrassment for the White House: "It's hard to find a case where a president has said something that was deliberately false to the American people and, when proven false, had to backpedal," observed one historian.[45]

Earlier in the day, the president had also testified under oath before a grand jury. There he explained his previous statements, from the Jones deposition, that he had not had sexual relations with Monica Lewinsky, nor persuaded her to lie. "These encounters did not consist of sexual intercourse," the president told prosecutors. "They did not constitute sexual relations, as I understood that term to be defined. . . . But they did involve inappropriate, intimate contact. . . . I regret that what began as a friendship came to include that conduct. And I take full responsibility for my actions." Clinton insisted that he had not lied in his deposition, but was simply trying to be unhelpful to Jones's lawyers. He chose his words carefully, saying his answer in one instance depended on what the definition of "is" is.

A month later, Republicans from the House Judiciary Committee made the president's videotaped testimony available to the media, which played clips continually throughout the week of September 21. Presidential adviser Paul Begala was among those glued to the television that week. "Watching that videotape was an uncomfortable but transforming event. I sat there all day . . . just mouth agape at the kinds of questions being asked."[46] Apparently, many Americans agreed with Begala. Polls showed that Clinton's job approval ratings had actually inched up, while the number of people favoring impeachment dropped a half-dozen percentage points.[47] The president's videotape testimony, it turns out, had the opposite effect of what some political foes may have been expecting. *Buffalo News* correspondent Douglas Turner explained that the "humiliating grilling . . . did not live up to its advance billing as a rare look at Clinton losing his composure, snarling, even stomping out of the room. Instead, viewers saw a composed and patient first witness, whose performance ranged from evasive to steely to combative."[48]

Between the president's August 17 message to the nation and the September 21 release of his videotaped grand jury testimony came another media bombshell: the Starr Report. The independent counsel's report to the House on September 9 contained what Starr called convincing evidence that the president had committed impeachable offenses. It also contained extremely graphic testimony, material so X-rated that one observer dubbed it "the most detailed pornographic government report in history."[49] Excerpts from Starr's report were immediately published in newspapers and magazines, while whole drafts were transmitted over the Internet and parts even read over television. Before long, several publishers issued the entire text in book form. Press Secretary Mike McCurry said he was particularly appalled by the salacious quality of the Internet transmission: It was "a horrific moment when all of the filters that are present in the world of journalism evaporated and you had raw information suddenly available in the mainstream."[50] Obviously, the administration's enchantment with unmediated forums had worn off since the 1992 campaign. Spin control was rendered almost futile, when Americans could read or hear the entire report for themselves. Still, White House spokespersons soldiered on.

Spin control was also more difficult amid the tidal wave of general media attention to the scandal. The "old media" alone were expending "prodigious" energy on it: "The Washington bureau of the Associated Press moved 4,109 stories on the scandal in [1998]. It had 25 reporters working regularly on the story. The *New York Times* had a dozen reporters on it, with another handful working on it in other cities."[51] Clearly, the magnitude of the assignment put an unusual strain on news organizations and the White House staff in charge of dealing with their demands.

McCurry's resignation had been announced in July, and now the time had arrived. On October 1, 1998, he held his last press briefing and confessed being drained from months of unceasing questions about the president's latest crisis. He told reporters that he had always tried to be truthful, but conceded that "frankly, the president misled me, too, so I came here and misled you on occasion."[52] He said he had tried to navigate honestly between both "combatants in this adversarial relationship," and defended his decision to shield himself from Clinton's thinking on the Lewinsky scandal.[53] His 539th briefing before the press was not, however, immune from tough questions. In answer to one by Sam Donaldson, about how twenty-five years earlier Bill Clinton had said that President Nixon deserved impeachment for lying to the American public, McCurry quashed the comparison. As usual, though, McCurry was calm and smooth. Indeed, despite being "the public face of a pained administration," the forty-three-year-old spokesman continued to joke with and charm those in attendance.[54] Tributes came immediately. "I don't think I'll ever see a better press secretary than Mike McCurry," wrote Godfrey Sperling of the *Christian Science Monitor* the next day. "How he ever dealt with all that prevarication from his boss and still was able to maintain his own credibility I'll never know."[55] Former press secretary Marlin Fitzwater noted a specific quality: "I suspect his presence on camera may be his greatest legacy."[56] Sam Donaldson intoned that McCurry was exiting with his reputation "intact," while National Public Radio's (NPR's) Mara Liasson contended that it had "even improved" somewhat.[57] Another lasting impression was the level of affection many reporters had for him. "McCurry's signal accomplishment," concluded Howard Kurtz, "is that after all the hand-to-hand combat with journalists, the late-night arguments and lectures on media sloppiness, most of the correspondents still love him."[58]

Many certainly did. But as there was considerable animosity directed at the president, some of that dissatisfaction was bound to trickle onto the press secretary's reputation. Notwithstanding Sam Donaldson and Mara Liasson's kind words for McCurry, not a few journalists were deeply disappointed with White House communication policy. Several editorials in the *New York Times*, for example, had gently scolded McCurry's modus operandi during the scandal, while others in the press went even further. Philip Terzian of the *Pittsburgh Post-Gazette* poked fun at McCurry for his see-no-evil "Sgt. Schultz Strategy" of knowing nothing when it counted. He then took the press secretary to task for his public timidity in sharing information, while behind the scenes engaging in normal "spin control: attacking Kenneth Starr, impugning the motives of witnesses, protecting Mr. Clinton from legitimate inquiries about the scandal. He could dish it out, but he wouldn't take it."[59]

Meanwhile, the president kept up selected public appearances, reserving as much distance from the scandal—and physical distance from journalists—as possible. "[I]n that long year of 1998," McCurry later said, "there would have been very little point in having a formal press conference unless you were prepared to stand there and take 30, 40, 50 questions on Monica Lewinsky."[60] Aides, of course, continued to fan out onto the daily round of television talk shows, defending Clinton, while severely criticizing Starr, congressional Republicans, and the press. "[T]here isn't a talk show out there," observed former press secretary Marlin Fitzwater, "where the Clinton White House doesn't have a spokesman on it, Lanny Davis or somebody, and they really have learned how to force their view, to go over the head of the press."[61] To stave off impeachment "the president's lawyers blanketed the Sunday talk shows."[62] Logistically, the constant "spin" game divided the administration, but realistically it distracted everyone. Part of the White House dealt exclusively with the controversy, while the rest of the administration did its best to disregard "the 800-pound Monica elephant in the middle of the room."[63] That task was made more challenging by votes in the House Judiciary Committee, then in the full House, to proceed with its impeachment investigation.

IMPEACHMENT

Despite the best efforts of the Clinton spin team to direct attention elsewhere and to attack the president's critics in and out of Congress, by mid-October the White House was in terrific danger. The media resounded with calls for Clinton's resignation; some 150 newspapers, in fact, concluding it was time for the president to step down. Equally bad was the relationship between the White House and the Washington press corps. McCurry's ambition to improve it had collapsed completely. "It was an abject failure. . . . I think the president still sees this adversarial relationship as an acrimonious one, and I guess I do, too," McCurry said after his last press conference.[64]

Not only was the press generally hostile towards the administration, but many in Congress were, too. The scandal had poisoned the mood in Washington, and the president's political opponents were beginning to close ranks. On December 19, 1998, the U.S. House of Representatives voted to impeach President Clinton on two counts: grand jury perjury (228 to 206) and obstruction of justice (221 to 212). The votes were close and conformed to party lines—just five Democrats and five Republicans had switched sides on the first article, for example. The outcome put the nation in a daze. Republicans appeared almost disoriented, while Democrats utterly reeled. Former presidential adviser George Stephanopoulos could only shake his head in wonder: "I would never have dreamed two things," he told a reporter. "I would never have dreamed that the country would have been so improved eight years into his stewardship. And I never dreamed of the day that I would wake up and see this morning's headline. Neither one can be erased."[65] Others were not so sure, and promised that Clinton would rebound from this, too. But first they had to wait for the increasingly tense, almost electric, spectacle taking place in the Congress.

During the second week of January 1999, President Clinton's impeachment trial in the Senate began. On January 14, the upper chamber heard arguments presented by the House managers, and all of Capitol Hill was engaged in battle. Meanwhile, press secretary Joe Lockhart was working harder than ever to quell journalistic brush fires. Less deferential to reporters than was McCurry, Lockhart grew more aggressive in and out of press briefings, sometimes calling network news correspondents seconds after the end of a particular report. CBS reporter Scott Pelley said that Lockhart's practice was even more noticeable in 1999. "We are getting more calls these days after the broadcast," Pelley said.[66] And though the president was no longer holding press conferences, his staff was busy on other fronts. The White House attended carefully to its website, for example, providing "pages and pages of Clinton-Gore accomplishments that 'transformed' the nation. Recently, the site also began featuring a trial brief defending Clinton against the two articles of impeachment being considered by the Senate."[67]

On February 12, the U.S. Senate voted to acquit President Clinton. All along, most experts doubted that congressional prosecutors would secure enough votes for conviction. They were right. The obstruction charge garnered fifty "ayes," the perjury charge only forty-five. Neither provided the two-thirds necessary to convict the president. The public seemed to have expected as much. As media critic Michael Gartner noted afterward, two million Americans had watched the acquittal on CNN that evening, while twice as many people had opted to watch professional wrestling on Turner Network Television (TNT) instead.[68] Thus, the most serious presidential crisis in a generation ended with a fitting aside: a motley assortment of media had fanned the scandal but also, at times, helped to obscure it.

CONCLUSION

President Clinton endured a number of personal crises in his eight years in the White House: a reopened Whitewater investigation, his administration's mishandling of FBI files, the travel office fiasco, Paula Jones's sexual harassment lawsuit, the Monica Lewinsky revelations, impeachment. These imbroglios plagued Bill Clinton's tenure in office and severely strained his relationship with the press. They fanned his "lasting animosity" toward journalists, his unshakable suspicion that the press was determined to destroy him.[69] Unfortunately, "Clinton's attitude toward the media did him much harm and by the time the [Lewinsky] scandal occurred, he had very few sympathizers in the press corps."[70] And sympathy among members of the "traditional" news media was still critical for effective presidential public relations. In a sense, then, his media dilemma during the '92 campaign was carried forth for the rest of the decade. Yet, so was his response to it. As in 1992, the president chose again in 1998 to go around the Washington press corps and mainstream journalists, and focus instead on alternative media, if only through underlings. Since the president of the United States is busy and must maintain the dignity of the office, Clinton simply deputized various aides and supporters to defend him in these new-news forums. So out went Rahm Emanuel, Lanny Davis, Greg Craig, or John Podesta to talk shows like *Larry King Live* or *Geraldo*. Aides could also appear in his behalf on conventional news programs and do interviews with the Washington press corps. "The genius of the White House spin artists," Howard Kurtz wrote, "has been not just in beating back scandalous headlines, but in finding ways to circumvent all those annoying journalists and connect with the public."[71] And, of course, the president also had Mike McCurry and Joe Lockhart.

Still, even through his subordinates, President Clinton could not set

the pace and tone and substance of countless hours of daily cable programming devoted to talk about his administration. Nor could anyone
keep track, much less influence, the vast universe that was the Internet.
Nineteen-ninety-eight was not like 1992. Alternative media were no
longer in their infancy but in a hormonally energized adolescence. That
latest phase also meant a closely entwined relationship between politics
and entertainment that closed certain opportunities while providing others. In February 1999, for example, the *New York Times* organized a
discussion between Mike McCurry, the president's former press secretary, and Liz Rosenberg, entertainer Madonna's chief spokesperson.[72]
Although each person had interesting things to say individually, neither
really seemed to be listening to the other, and the result was not much
of a conversation. The very idea that these two individuals were juxtaposed in the same forum, however, speaks volumes. Their meeting underscored the conflation of politics and entertainment, as did the fact that
Monica Lewinsky's first attorney, William Ginsburg, became in the winter of 1998 "the most sought after television talk show guest."[73]

Politics and entertainment may have had one thing in common in the
1990s, though: a propensity for blab. "Never before has gossip been so
golden," one journalist said.[74] Howard Kurtz explained the new media
environment this way: "Bill Clinton dwelt in the same murky precincts
of celebrity as Dennis Rodman, Courtney Love, and David Letterman.
In a hundred-channel world the president had become just another piece
of programming to be marketed, and high ratings were hardly guaranteed."[75] Indeed, wrote Josh Getlin of the *Los Angeles Times*, "the same
voyeuristic culture that elevated [Clinton] has now tarnished his legacy,
perhaps irrevocably."[76] It turns out that in a culture in which "character
and celebrity are blurred in the media,"[77] in which a certain measure of
notoriety is essentially good because it brings focus in a confusing and
otherwise distracting world, presidential scandal today cuts two ways: it
can, perversely, enhance popularity, while in the long term diminish
respect. This is, needless to say, not the historical pattern, which is more
nearly the opposite, as subsequent generations tend to treat presidential
misbehavior more charitably. Maximum exposure still exacts a high cost,
then, but, but the price is probably paid later rather than sooner. Some
students of presidential communications, in fact, have questioned
whether a lot of talk is a good thing for an administration, temporarily,
or otherwise. Too much discourse can invite more criticism than would
otherwise occur on its own. And too much informality can effectively
remove the protective layer that political leaders have traditionally drawn

strength behind.[78] As one writer asked rhetorically, "He who lives by the talk show dies by it?"[79] Well, almost, in Clinton's case. He certainly suffered because of these media. Indeed, he might be "the most publicly shamed president of modern time."[80] But ironically the insulation of informality which these forums provided may have saved his presidency by making the scandal and even impeachment seem unreal, less important, irrelevant, or ridiculous. And therefore the price of remaining in the White House may likely be that Clinton leaves behind a cartoonish legacy.

NOTES

1. Chris Bury, "The Clinton Years," ABC, *Nightline* (January 8, 2001).

2. Project for Excellence in Journalism, *Changing Definitions of News: A Look at the Mainstream Press over 20 Years* (March 6, 1998); cited in "Ticker," *Brill's Content* (July/August 1998), p. 152.

3. Ibid.

4. George Clooney, "Just Tell Us the Truth," *Brill's Content* (July/August 1998), pp. 80–81.

5. Paul J. Quirk, "Scandal Time: The Clinton Impeachment and the Distraction of American Politics," in *The Clinton Scandal and the Future of American Government*, ed. Mark J. Rozell and Clyde Wilcox (Washington, DC: Georgetown University Press, 2000), p. 129–30.

6. James Lull and Stephen Hinerman, "The Search for Scandal," in *Media Scandals: Morality and Desire in the Popular Culture Marketplace*, ed. Lull and Hinerman (New York: Columbia University Press, 1997), p. 125.

7. Juan Rodriguez, "The Power of Blather," *Montreal Gazette* (February 8, 1998), p. D1.

8. See, for example, the following editorial, "History Will View Clinton Legacy Favorably," *Atlanta Journal and Constitution* (January 19, 2001), p. A22.

9. "Perils of Paula," *The Nation* (May 30, 1994), p. 733.

10. Susan Estrich, "Feminists Needn't Defend Paula Jones," *USA Today* (May 12, 1994), p. A11.

11. Katha Pollitt, "Subject to Debate," *The Nation* (June 13, 1994), p. 824.

12. Stuart Taylor, "Her Case against Clinton," *The American Lawyer* (November 1996), p. 56.

13. Debra Saunders, "Welcome, Anita," *San Francisco Chronicle* (November 24, 1996), p. 9.

14. Evan Thomas with Michael Isikoff, "Clinton versus Paula Jones," *Newsweek* (January 13, 1997), p. 26.

15. Steven Brill, "Pressgate," *Brill's Content* (July/August 1998), p. 131.

16. Steven Brill, "Pressgate," p. 151. Kenneth Starr quickly questioned Brill's motives. He said he formerly regarded Steven Brill as a friend and claimed that Brill had set him up, by talking with him under false pretenses and taking his comments out of context, in order to launch his new magazine—an accusation Brill strongly denies. For more on this feud, see Bob Woodward, *Shadow: Five Presidents and the Legacy of Watergate* (New York: Simon & Schuster, 1999), p. 405.

17. Michael Gartner, "How the Monica Story Played in Mid-America," *Columbia Journalism Review* (May/June 1999), p. 34.

18. James Stewart, *Blood Sport: The President and His Adversaries* (New York: Simon & Schuster, 1996; Touchstone, 1997), pp. 447, 421.

19. Bob Woodward, *Shadow: Five Presidents and the Legacy of Watergate* (New York: Simon & Schuster, 1999), pp. 515–16.

20. This figure is based on a Nexis database search of "Monica Lewinsky" for the thirty-one days of January 1998.

21. Gene Lyons, quoted in Maureen Dowd, "President Irresistible," *New York Times* (February 18, 1998), p. A21.

22. Sam Donaldson, ABC, *This Week* (January 25, 1998).

23. Howard Kurtz, *Spin Cycle: Inside the Clinton Propaganda Machine* (New York: Free Press, 1998), p. xiv.

24. Howard Kurtz, "In the Hot Seat of Power," *Washington Post* (September 9, 1998), p. D1.

25. Elizabeth Shogren, "Spinmeister McCurry Leaving the Podium," *Los Angeles Times* (July 24, 1998), p. A22.

26. Mike McCurry, quoted in "McCurry in 'Doghouse' over Remarks," *Minneapolis Star Tribune* (February 18, 1998), p. A4.

27. John Carlin, *Independent* (February 18, 1998), p. 10.

28. Editorial, "The McCurry Confessions," *New York Times* (February 19, 1998), p. A18.

29. Helen Thomas, quoted in Susan Baer, "Clinton Spokesman Has the Last Word," *Baltimore Sun* (July 24, 1998), p. A1.

30. "A Spinner's Unmerited Praise," *New York Times* (July 25, 1998), p. A12.

31. Allan Miller, "Willey's Credibility Takes Hits," *Los Angeles Times* (March 22, 1998), p. A1.

32. Larry Speakes, on CNN, *Larry King Live* (March 24, 1998).

33. Molly W. Andolina and Clyde Wilcox, "Pubilc Opinion: The Paradoxes of Clinton's Personality," in *The Clinton Scandal and the Future of American Government*, ed. Mark J. Rozell and Clyde Wilcox (Washington, DC: Georgetown University Press, 2000), p. 175.

34. David W. Moore, "Americans Back Dismissal of Paula Jones' Lawsuit," *Gallup Poll Monthly* 391 (April 1998), p. 2.

35. Frank Newport and Alec Gallup, "Clinton's Popularity Paradox," *Gallup Poll Monthly* 388 (January 1998), p. 14.

36. Jules Witcover, "Where We Went Wrong," *Columbia Journalism Review* (March/April 1998), p. 19.

37. Elizabeth Shogren, "Spinmeister McCurry Leaving the Podium," p. A22.

38. Lloyd Grove, "Places, Everyone! 'Intern Story,' Act 3, Scene 2; Monica Gets Immunity, and Mike McCurry Gets Ontological," *Washington Post* (July 29, 1998), p. D1.

39. Quoted in Lloyd Grove, "Places, Everyone! 'Intern Story,' Act 3, Scene 2; Monica Gets Immunity, and Mike McCurry Gets Ontological," *Washington Post* (July 29, 1998), p. D1.

40. Roxanne Roberts, "Marlin Fitzwater: Well Done," *Washington Post* (June 24, 1998), p. D1.

41. Clinton, quoted on CNBC, *Tim Russert* (March 13, 1999).

42. "McCurry Leaving White House," *Washington Post*; reprinted in *Minneapolis Star Tribune* (July 24, 1998), p. A4.

43. Elizabeth Shogren, "Spinmeister McCurry Leaving the Podium," p. A22.

44. Senator Dianne Feinstein, quoted in Jill Lawrence, "Next on Presidential Agenda: Restoring Credibility," *USA Today* (August 19, 1998), p. A5.

45. Michael Beschloss, quoted in Jill Lawrence, "Next on Presidential Agenda: Restoring Credibility," *USA Today* (August 19, 1998), p. A5.

46. Paul Begala, quoted in "The Clinton Years," ABC, *Nightline* (January 11, 2001).

47. David W. Moore, "Clinton Support Strong after Release of Grand Jury Tapes," *Gallup Poll Monthly* 396 (September 1998), p. 12.

48. Douglas Turner, "Spectacle Seems to Sway Few as TV Airs Clinton Testimony," *Buffalo News* (September 22, 1998), p. A1.

49. Woodward, *Shadow*, p. 464.

50. Mike McCurry, quoted in Joanne Ostrow, "Clinton Media Dissected," *Denver Post* (February 22, 1999), p. E5.

51. Michael Gartner, "How the Monica Story Played in Mid-America," p. 34.

52. Quoted in Amy Baer, "Clinton Spokesman McCurry Bows Out to Media Applause," *San Diego Union-Tribune* (October 2, 1998), p. A12.

53. Susan Baer, "McCurry Leaves with Reputation, Humor Intact," *Baltimore Sun* (October 2, 1998), p. A3.

54. Mimi Hall, "McCurry Speaks for White House for the Last Time," *USA Today* (October 2, 1998), p. A5.

55. Godfrey Sperling, "The Persuasive Mr. Lockhart," *Christian Science Monitor* (September 28, 1999), p. 21.

56. Marlin Fitzwater, quoted in Associated Press, "Outgoing Press Secretary McCurry Is Viewed as Steadying Influence," *St. Louis Post-Dispatch* (September 29, 1998), p. A2.

57. Sam Donaldson, quoted in Susan Baer, "McCurry Leaves with Reputa-

tion, Humor Intact," *Baltimore Sun* (October 2, 1998), p. A3; Mara Liasson, National Public Radio, *Morning Edition* (October 2, 1998).

58. Howard Kurtz, "White House Spokesman's Final Turn," *Washington Post* (October 2, 1998), p. D1.

59. Philip Terzian, "Mike McCurry Knew What Not to Know; He Was Clinton's Sgt. Schultz," *Pittsburgh Post-Gazette* (October 13, 1998), p. A11. The following year, television host Bernard Kalb chided McCurry for his attitude: "The luxury of not wanting to know does not fit in with the requirements of a press spokesman. You must know, and if you cannot coexist with knowing then you have to leave." Kalb, CNN, *Reliable Sources* (August 7, 1999).

60. Mike McCurry, on CNBC, *Tim Russert* (March 13, 1999).

61. Marlin Fitzwater, ibid.

62. Woodward, *Shadow*, p. 464.

63. Mike McCurry, quoted in Joanne Ostrow, "Clinton Media Dissected," p. E5.

64. Mike McCurry, quoted in Mara Liasson, "McCurry Steps Down," National Public Radio, *Morning Edition* (October 2, 1998).

65. George Stephanopoulos, quoted in Adam Nagourney, "Impeachment: The Class of '92," *New York Times* (December 21, 1998), p. A22.

66. Scott Pelley, quoted in Howard Kurtz, "The Full Retort," *Washington Post* (January 18, 1999), p. C1.

67. Jeff Barker, "McCurry Remains Loyal to Clinton," *Arizona Republic* (January 17, 1999), p. A24.

68. Michael Gartner, "How the Monica Story Played in Mid-America," p. 34.

69. Stewart, *Blood Sport*, p. 198; Dick Morris, *Behind the Oval Office: Winning the Presidency in the Nineties* (New York: Random House, 1997), p. 99.

70. Mark J. Rozell and Clyde Wilcox, "The Clinton Presidency and the Politics of Scandal, in *The Clinton Scandal and the Future of American Government*, ed. Rozell and Wilcox (Washington, DC: Georgetown University Press, 2000), p. xx.

71. Howard Kurtz, "Plotting for Mr. President," *The Guardian* (October 19, 1998), p. 2; reprinted in Kurtz, *Spin Cycle: Inside the Clinton Propaganda Machine* (New York: Free Press, 1998).

72. Kevin Gray (moderator), "The Way We Live Now," *New York Times* VI (February 21, 1999), p. 26.

73. Woodward, *Shadow*, p. 397.

74. John Farmer, "If You Want Loyalty, Get a Dog," *New Orleans Times-Picayune* (March 14, 1999), p. B7.

75. Howard Kurtz, *Spin Cycle*, p. xxiii.

76. Josh Getlin, "Clinton under Fire; Clinton Legacy May Be History, Say Historians," *Los Angeles Times* (August 19, 1998), p. A16. Getlin interviewed

scholars Robert Dallek, Arthur J. Schlesinger, Jr., Alan Brinkley, Joyce Appleby, and Joan Hoff.

77. Bruce E. Gronbeck, "Character, Celebrity, and Sexual Innuendo in the Mass-Mediated Presidency," in *Media Scandals: Morality and Desire in the Popular Culture Marketplace*, ed. James Lull and Stephen Hinerman (New York: Columbia University Press, 1997), p. 125.

78. Craig Allen Smith, "Rough Stretches and Honest Disagreements: Is Bill Clinton Redefining the Rhetorical Press?" in Robert E. Denton, Jr., and Rachel L. Holloway (eds.), *The Clinton Presidency: Images, Issues, and Communication Strategies* (Westport, CT: Praeger Publishers, 1996), p. 243; Robert E. Denton, Jr., and Rachel L. Holloway, "Clinton and the Town Hall Meetings: Mediated Conversation and the Risk of Being 'In Touch,' " in Ibid., p. 37.

79. Juan Rodriguez, "The Power of Blather," p. D1.

80. Andolina and Wilcox, p. 171.

6

Surrealism

INTRODUCTION

The spectacle of Internet sites devoted to his political demise or filled with page after page of embarrassing transcripts must have been astonishing to the president, but also rather ironic considering his successful piggybacking of alternative media in 1992. Here was a politician who had climbed his way to the top because of unconventional public forums and now stood in danger of being toppled by them. Still another, equally interesting relationship between Clinton and the mass media had become clear by the end of the 1990s. The image and legacy of President Clinton were inspiring thinly veiled depictions in film, some more veiled than others, some more complimentary than others. At times in this maelstrom of surrealism it was difficult to distinguish the authentic from the imaginary, and Americans sometimes found themselves wondering whether life really did imitate art.

Bill Clinton's earliest celluloid influence was evident in 1992, when personal friend and Hollywood producer Linda Bloodworth-Thomason put together a short but powerful campaign film for the Democratic candidate: "The Man From Hope." Subtle, polished, even moving, the political reel conveyed the dramatic breadth of Clinton's life and career, including such visual gems as his inspiring handshake with boyhood idol, President John F. Kennedy. It was an impressive piece of propaganda.

"The opposition party and even those within President George Bush's campaign staff were reportedly 'wowed' by the film's emotive power," one scholar recalled.[1] A fascinating political figure was thereby transformed into an ideal, a role model, an aspiration: Clinton the man elevated to the status of Clinton the allegory. Movie makers took notice.

The 1992 campaign itself generated a film documentary entitled *The War Room*, produced by D. A. Pennebaker and Chris Hegedus and released in 1993. An intense, seemingly minute-by-minute look inside Clinton headquarters, the film focused on the colorful campaign staff leaders and the way they handled both routine duties and unexpected crises. These operatives' main objectives were to be fast, efficient, and aggressive—to meet any attack almost simultaneously with one of their own. These are political soldiers, and they demonstrate a fierce determination to stay "on message," to avoid being distracted by opponents' ploys or by media sieges, to keep up the pressure, sustain the momentum, and remain positive but also on the offensive. What the documentary does best, though, is to convey the heavy emotional toll imposed by the campaign. We see the shouts and smiles during a primary victory, the fury during a disagreement, tears during a farewell speech. This is a genuine glimpse backstage, and it is often quite dramatic. Not surprisingly, *The War Room* made minor celebrities of George Stephanopolous and James Carville, both of whom inspired fictional characters at the cinema and on television, and both of whom afterward received innumerable invitations to appear on TV news talk shows and panel discussions.

The War Room was a hot commodity in the year following the election, a well-made, useful, and intriguing piece of filmmaking. But in many respects the most memorable and trenchant story about the 1992 campaign was told not in a documentary, but in a piece of fiction called *Primary Colors*, a picture based on the novel published anonymously in 1996 and later revealed to be the work of *Newsweek* writer Joe Klein.

PRIMARY COLORS

The identity of the anonymous author of the novel *Primary Colors* was probably the biggest American literary puzzle of the 1990s—and one of the biggest literary successes, too: In its first year, it went through about twenty printings and sold more than a million hardcover copies. All people could talk about in newspapers, magazines, and on television, it seemed, was who the mysterious author was. Guesses ranged from Henry Kissinger to Gary Trudeau and included just about every major journalist or politically active writer. "Whether intended or not, anonymity of authorship seemed key to the work's phenomenal success. The guessing game for a while became something of a national obsession, especially among TV 'talking heads.' "[2] Then, in May 1996, a Shakespearean scholar at Vassar published an article naming Joe Klein the "primary culprit."[3] Klein denied the charge, even screamed at friends that it wasn't him.[4] "I believed that I had a right to write an anonymous novel," he said later.[5] Finally, the *Washington Post* obtained an original manuscript copy of the novel in July and matched Klein's handwriting in the margin notes with a second sample. Until then, journalists were sure of only one thing: the unknown writer had superb access to and unparalleled inside information about the Clinton campaign. Everyone at the time knew that the presidential candidate in the book, Governor Stanton, was a somewhat more exaggerated version of Governor Clinton. As the title of a *Newsweek* article expressed the speculation, "Who Wrote the Book on Bill?"[6]

The characters and plot in *Primary Colors* were barely distinguishable from their real-life models: a mainly young but talented crew of politicos help elect a young and talented candidate whose extramarital sexual appetite is exceeded only by his and his wife's political ambition. In the film, Henry Burton (Adrian Lester), the young, squeaky-clean, idealistic son of a civil rights leader, and Richard Jemmons (Billy Bob Thornton), an older, wilder, raunchy southerner, are the primary odd couple determined to elect Jack Stanton (John Travolta) president. Jack is the governor of a small southern state, and a compassionate man who, however, constantly cheats on his wife, Susan (played by Emma Thompson). Like candidate Clinton, candidate Stanton eluded the draft during the Vietnam War and smoked marijuana while in college. He also endured an embarrassing episode reminiscent of the public allegations made by Gennifer Flowers in 1992: a longtime affair with a woman named Cashmere McCleod, who reveals tape-recorded phone messages of their conversations after the governor initially denied the relationship. Klein also injects the Whitewater scandal into the picture, but chooses another candidate to carry that particular political baggage and calls it "Tidewater." (Evidently, the screenwriter, Elaine May, did not want to put an improbably large number of skeletons in the main character's closet.) Rounding out the cast of key characters are Stanton damage-control specialist Libby Holden (Kathy Bates) and one of Stanton's primary opponents, Governor Fred Picker (Larry Hagman).

As in *The War Room*, the major players in *Primary Colors* put out frequent fires but also go on the offensive whenever possible. Henry and Libby travel to Miami looking for dirt on Governor Picker and come back with a couple of career-destroying surprises. Picker, it turns out, used cocaine years ago in the governor's mansion and also had a homosexual relationship with his drug supplier. They do not know, however, whether the Stantons will choose to use the information or bury it on behalf of a man they believe is basically decent and honorable. The Stantons don't hesitate at all; they leap at the idea of using the information against Picker. The Stantons' decision is devastating for Burton and Holden, Holden in particular, since she has known the Stantons for decades and once even asked Jack about using dirty tricks in 1972: "You remember, Jack? 'We gotta be able to do that, too.' And you said, 'No. Our job is to END all that. Our job is to make it clean. Because if it's clean, we win—because our ideas are better.' You remember that, Jack?"

The Picker episode is a central one in the movie, but more prominent are the many instances of Governor Stanton's indiscretions and infidelities, which seem so at odds with his genuine concern for and commitment to ordinary Americans. Stanton, a film critic explained, "is a flawed and contradictory man, baffling and hypnotic in his seamless combination of genuine caring with casual manipulation."[7] As Klein wrote of the governor in the novel, "He'll flash that famous misty look of his. And he will mean it."[8] Clinton, too, has earned a reputation for being both crafty and sincerely caring. As a politician, he misses no trick; as a mensch, he really likes being around other people. Stanton has one other prominent characteristic: a penchant for adulterous womanizing. From Cashmere McLeod to the literacy teacher to a teenage girl, Stanton has trouble keeping his pants on. Progressive causes never get in the way of his libido. The lech and the liberal, then, are the competing Jekyll-and-Hyde halves of Stanton's personality, a combination that has often been attributed to President Clinton as well.

The deft way Klein structured the plot, and the finesse with which screenwriter Elaine May and director Mike Nichols handled the characters, all make *Primary Colors* a brilliant piece of work. Ranking it alongside Robert Penn Warren's *All the King's Men* (which was itself a fictionalized account of Governor Huey Long's career), political media consultant Michael P. Shea says *Primary Colors* is an indispensable window into Clinton's election to the presidency: "[It] was, and remains, the most in-depth and accurate account of Bill Clinton's remarkable victory in 1992. Yes, as fiction it contained fabricated events and characters. But Klein's portrayal of the brilliant, calculating, morally flawed but genuinely compassionate Governor Stanton and his partner/victim/spouse rings truer and delves deeper than any news article or historical biography."[9] So true and so deep, apparently, that Shea confessed he sometimes confuses elements from the book and movie with those from real life: "*Primary Colors* was so good that today I sometimes find myself unclear as to which events actually happened and which were Klein's creations."[10]

Clinton himself has compounded the confusion. After the movie came out, the president actually invited John Travolta to a White House dinner to "perform" the role of Jack Stanton privately. Travolta said no: "I thought it was best to leave the character on screen and not do parties."[11] In some ways, too, the fictionalized version of President Clinton's life has been eerily superseded by actual developments. Says film critic Kenneth Turan: "As risqué as its speculations seemed when Klein was still anonymous, the rush of history, epitomized by the tale of Monica Lewinsky, has overtaken and surpassed what's been put on the screen."[12]

In any case, the characterizations hit close to home, and many of the real-life models publicly disassociated themselves from the film. James Carville, for example, emphatically distinguished himself from the character of Richard Jemmons. "When you see Bill Bob Thornton on the screen, it's not me. It's fiction."[13] Stephanopoulos also underscored the film's imaginative qualities, though he was said to be "obsessed" with the authorship of the book.[14] Certainly, no one doubted where Joe Klein got his inspiration for Jack Stanton. Klein covered the Clinton campaign closely for *Newsweek* in 1992. He published the novel anonymously in 1996, and he was given an abrupt leave-of-absence from the magazine when it was discovered he was the author, because he had denied the rumor so publicly and so emphatically. New York governor Mario Cuomo criticized Klein for his insulting portrayal of the character Ozio, the Italian American leader of a large northern state. Finally, a New York literacy teacher sued Klein for implying she had sex with then governor Clinton because the character she allegedly inspired on the screen had sex with Governor Stanton.[15] If the book was primarily a work of fiction, many real-life people who resembled its characters did not think so.

There were more strange connections between the real and the surreal: screenwriter Elaine May and director Mike Nichols had campaigned for Clinton in 1992; they even promised people close to the White House that the film would not embarrass the president. "It's secretly Seinfeld, it's about pals on the road . . . It's the happiest time of their lives."[16] Nichols nonetheless tried to hire Dee Dee Myers, James Carville, and

George Stephanopoulos as consultants for the film, Myers in particular. All of them declined. Billy Bob Thornton was a personal friend of Clinton's; the two had a mutual friend in fellow Arkansan Harry Thomason. Therefore, the line between fiction and reality was blurred throughout production of the movie, and both political and cinematic enthusiasts must have watched in amazement as people purportedly sympathetic to Clinton proceeded to make a movie almost sure to roast him.

WAG THE DOG

The 1997 film *Wag the Dog* may have provided the most surreal experience in twentieth-century presidential history. The movie, based on the novel *American Hero* by Larry Beinhart, is about a political consultant, Conrad Brean (Robert DeNiro), whose solution for a president beleaguered by sexual scandal is to concoct a phony war between the United States and Albania. "What did the Albanians do to us?" asks White House aide Winifred Ames (Anne Heche). "What did the Albanians do *for* us?" Brean fires back. As laughable as this exchange is, Brean does deliver a war and delivers it convincingly. This "virtual conflict" is manufactured by film producer Stanley Motss (Dustin Hoffman), who with Brean cooks up the right visual images, songs, and slogans to give the charade credibility. They also exploit media skepticism by denying what no one has yet asked—that there is a B3 Bomber program, for example. Their efforts work. It turns out that when a politician denies something often enough, journalists come to believe it's true. Through such creative manipulation, delivered at just the right time, they squeeze out criticism of the president until after the election. Americans rally behind the commander in chief during the perceived foreign crisis, while the allegations by a young girl that the president engaged in sexual misconduct are forgotten.

Viewers never learn whether the allegations are actually true, just as in real life we rarely find out the merits of various rumors. The fact is, unfortunately, it often doesn't matter. So when Ames asks Brean if he'd like to know if the charges are true, the political guru says the question's irrelevant. "What difference does it make if it's true? It's a story . . . they're going to run with it." And he's right—the media do run with it, until they're thrown off the trail by his agenda-setting creativity: a wild-goose chase that ultimately leads nowhere. As many film critics noted at the time, it was a smart if paper-thin premise, "the characters . . . not so much real people as elements in a single, elaborate gag,"[17] and therefore the story line plods along at times.

Still, the movie's satiric insights—that politics and entertainment are so entwined as to confuse and mislead; that government leaders resort to any degree of trickery to stay in power; that cynicism runs rife through the media—are incisive. "[G]iven recent events," movie reviewer Thelma Adams wrote in December 1997, "the dark comedy that fuses Hollywood, electoral politics and image consultants doesn't seem as far-fetched as it might have four years ago."[18] But Adams was speaking in generalities at that point. Subsequent events proved even more unnerving.

Early in 1998, rumors surfaced about an extramarital affair between the president and a White House intern. Then came the public allegations. Amid simultaneous talk of trouble abroad with Iraq, *Wag the Dog* suddenly appeared "eerily prescient." The movie, noted a sharp observer, "also has a TV news clip of the fictional president greeting the girl at a function—the scene bears an uncanny resemblance to the now-infamous clip of Clinton hugging . . . Lewinsky, right down to the black beret worn by the girl in the film."[19] *Time* printed a brief blow-by-blow contrast:

Movie: Offscreen, President fondles "firefly girl" in back room of White House.

Real Life: On tape, intern allegedly recounts tales of oral sex with President in back room of White House.

Movie: Events in Albania distract nation from scandal.

Real Life: Scandal distracts nation from events in Cuba, Ireland and Iraq.

Movie: Mr. Political-Fix-It (DeNiro) is brought in to manage scandal.

Real Life: Mr. Political-Fix-It (Jordan) is accused of being part of scandal.

Movie: President makes it through crisis to happy ending.

Real Life: Well, this ain't Hollywood.[20]

Even the film's director, Barry Levinson, proclaimed tongue-in-cheek, "Hey, we were just kidding."[21] By August, though, the film appeared to have been an outright omen. Seventy-two hours after apologizing for lying about his affair with White House intern Monica Lewinsky, President Clinton announced that the U.S. had bombed sites in Sudan and Afghanistan. Even General Henry Shelton, the chairman of the Joint Chiefs of Staff, later called the timing "absolutely incredible." Critics again began comparing events with those in the recent *Wag the Dog*, shaking their heads at the "striking similarities" between the two.[22] All the commentary stimulated videotape rentals of the movie, which suddenly became a cultural phenomenon at the time.

The film also got entangled with foreign policy and became a dangerous impediment, both for the president and for concerned citizens alike. An editorial in *USA Today*, for example, pleaded with Americans not to let the film "stall action against Saddam."[23] It was a no-win situation for Clinton. If he did nothing vis-à-vis Iraq, he would appear weak. If he acted, he would be branded a self-centered manipulator, one who took the crassest of cues from Tinseltown pictures. Hollywood had so perceptively imagined Washington that the president had to steer clear of any further coincidences. He could not afford to let his actions mirror those in the movie without incurring considerable moral and political condemnation. It was an unprecedented situation: a film effectively tying the hands of the leader of the free world.

That episode wasn't the last in which the movie made news. In the spring of 1999, Serb television ran the film repeatedly to alert people to the opportunism of American political strategy and to stir up anti-American sentiment.[24] *Wag the Dog* thus began as art and wound up a political tool, was transformed from entertainment into propaganda, an American tale into an international icon. *Wag the Dog* brought Hollywood close enough to Washington to make even studio executives uncomfortable. It made many journalists uneasy, too. Reporters' questions on the topic, however gingerly raised, were always, if understandably, cooly ignored. Some, writers such as the leftist writer Christopher Hitchens, are still convinced that President Clinton conducted a foreign policy partially derived from personal reasons.[25] Conservative writers share that cynicism. In mid-1999, for example, Paul Burgess said he believed in "Clinton's seeming tendency to profile his wars against his scandals. . . . There has to be some concrete reason for William Jefferson Clinton's amazing transfiguration these last 18 months from the persona of Hawkeye Pierce to that of George S. Patton."[26]

THE CONTENDER

If *Primary Colors* and *Wag the Dog* were both detrimental to Bill Clinton's reputation, *The Contender* was meant to provide Democratic rehabilitation. Released in October 2000, *The Contender* was written by Los Angeles film critic Rod Lurie and starred Joan Allen as Laine Hanson, a Democrat senator from New England who is nominated for the vice presidency and run through the mud by vicious Republican opponents. Their leader is Shelly Runyon (Gary Oldham), a friend of the president's second choice, but more importantly a petty partisan politician who wastes no time expressing his disdain for Hanson, her stature, and her politics. Runyon launches an all-out smear campaign against the female nominee and eventually uncovers allegations that she had participated in a drunken orgy while in college.

The bulk of the movie consists of Hanson's struggle to endure the embarrassing public allegations and demeaning confirmation hearings. The Senate Republicans, Runyon in particular, appear to take delight in roughly interrogating the nominee, provoking her to anger, humiliating her with coy innuendo and shameless gossip-mongering. Hanson chooses not to answer any question of a sexual nature, saying such matters are none of the committee's business and utterly irrelevant to confirmation. The president is increasingly uncomfortable that his nominee is taking such a beating, and he is under pressure to drop her and go with his second choice, a person sure to be confirmed. So the movie is secondarily about his struggle. But both his and Hanson's battles are really one and the same—the battle between political courage and simple expediency. Is the president brave enough to stand by his first choice? Is Hanson brave enough to weather partisan persecution?

The Contender is a transparent Democratic parable of the Clinton impeachment hearings, the story that many members of that political party would no doubt like to believe best summarizes the whole Monica Lewinsky scandal: a personal affair of no relevance to public discussion, least of all to debates about removing the president from office. Hanson and Runyon are continually contrasted in heavy-handed fashion: she an attractive, all-American blonde who jogs and eats vegetarian; he a small, homely man who looks like a weasel and indulges his appetites for fat stogies and bloody red beef steaks. Worse than his personal habits, though, are his irrational bigotries and hatreds. He is a Republican witch-hunter, who seems to take a perverse pleasure in exposing and then humiliating sinners. Oldham gives more depth to the character than the average actor would have been able, but Runyon is clearly the villain of the film and we are not supposed to find him appealing in any way.

Hanson, by contrast, is brave, selfless, and principled. Her refusal to answer virtually every question about her sexual history (with one puzzling exception) because she says it's not relevant to the confirmation hearings seems to be a kind of combination of the Hollywood mystique about blacklisted Communist artists during the 1950s and, of course, Democratic wisdom concerning the Clinton impeachment hearings. Interestingly, the latter comes up in the movie when Hanson is asked whether, as a senator, she voted to impeach President Clinton. She did, she testifies, but explains that she voted that way because Clinton was commander in chief and ought to be held accountable for extramarital misconduct in the same way that military officers are. Direct criticism of Clinton then? Perhaps. Conservative film critic John Simon maintains the movie "is not about liberals versus conservatives, Democrats versus Republicans, good guys versus bad guys. Still less is it, as some will undoubtedly suggest, some sort of apology for Bill Clinton—quite the contrary. Rather, the film sees gray areas in good people and humanity in not-so-good ones, but believes in the ultimate decency of human-kind."[27]

Where is the good in Runyon's character? In fact, none of Hanson's Republican opposition comes off well, so I cannot imagine to what po-litical balance Simon is referring. Indeed, given the black-and-white por-trait of Democrats and Republicans in the movie, and considering the resemblance of the story line to actual events between 1998 and 1999, it seems more likely that screenwriter Lurie is attempting to distance his character from Clinton in order to give her more credibility, in order to give the moral message in the picture more weight. Lurie thus sacrifices the external details of the Clinton impeachment in order to redeem "sin-ners" of Clinton's stripe. Sexual peccadillos, the film concludes, ought to remain private matters beyond the jurisdiction of public bodies. In retrospect, then, *The Contender* works to salvage President Clinton's reputation by suggesting that he was persecuted for a small, private affair of trivial consequence, because ruthless partisans were determined to destroy him.

CONCLUSION

Primary Colors, Wag the Dog, and *The Contender* were far from the only movies about the presidency during the 1990s. Indeed, no other decade ever witnessed so many. The list includes *Absolute Power, Air Force One, The American President, Dave, Deterrence, Dick, Indepen-dence Day, Jefferson in Paris, J.F.K., Mars Attacks!, Murder at 1600, My Fellow Americans, Nixon,* and *Thirteen Days.*

Television, too, had caught the bug. In 1999, NBC began airing a dramatic series for television called *West Wing*—about a young, pro-gressive, and photogenic president—which by the end of its first season had proved a huge success.[28] Producers of the Comedy Central cartoon

South Park announced in 2000 that they were preparing a television sitcom about White House life called *Family First*. And, of course, TV shows occasionally made direct reference to President Clinton himself. Home Box Office's (HBO's) smash hit *The Sopranos*, for example, featured a brief family discussion one morning. In it, the daughter complained about what she described as the president's persecution until her father angrily warned her not to talk about sex during breakfast.

Clearly, the American media were fascinated by the personal side of the presidency during the Clinton administration. Was it coincidence? Probably not. And the title of George Stephanopoulos's best-selling book about his former boss's rise to the top, *All Too Human*, suggests why. The story of Bill Clinton is itself fascinating, perhaps because it has been so picturesque and dramatic and, yes, human—so human that for opponents he's the obvious villain of a morality play, for supporters the martyr in a political parable (about how public officials who believe in the "right" principles must often bear crosses). On a simpler level, Clinton has "demystified" the office. "We see him with human frailties," Rod Lurie explains, with "weight gains, an extramarital affair or affairs. It's really made him the very first president we can identify with not necessarily as a regular guy, but a guy filled with foibles."[29]

The recent glut in "presidential cinema" may also be the product of a decade characterized by prosperous yuppies thirsty for celebrity gossip and intrigued by their political counterparts. As Terrence Rafferty has written, the "target audience for this new style of Oval Office drama is not those who want to be Bill Clinton, but those who dream of being George Stephanopoulos."[30] According to Rafferty, Hollywood has in the 1990s been obsessed with the powerbrokers behind the scenes—the Carvilles and Matalins—rather than the chief executive himself, which is why in a movie such as *The Contender*, for example, the president is rarely as interesting as the people around him.

But that explanation still does not fully suffice, for it fails to take into account many movies' obvious and not-so-obvious references to the Clinton administration. Clearly, our 42nd president has had something to do with that influence. First of all, Clinton's affection for West Coast glitterati has probably also stimulated interest. As a film critic recalled, "In the first weeks of the Clinton administration, the Hollywood stampede to the nation's capital was so heavy, veterans quipped: 'On a clear day in Washington, you can see Barbra Streisand forever.' "[31] To cite but one example, Clinton arranged to get reporter's credentials for actress Anna Deavere Smith, who played a presidential assistant on the big

screen in *The American President*, in order for Smith to ride on Air
Force One.[32] More significantly, his fabled ambition, prodigious appetites, impressive talents, and rumored weaknesses were all well docu-
mented during his two terms in office, and great men struggling with
earthly temptations is, as we know, storyteller's gold. At least one writer,
however, has doubted that Hollywood could ever truly capture Bill Clinton (or his wife, for that matter), because Clinton was such a consummate
showman: "But if writers and actors can't do it, the Clintons can. They
are the artists and the art. Some of what they do may be embarrassing,
but, true to their 1960s roots, the Clintons are performance artists of the
highest order."[33] Others have thought so, too. As theatre critic Robert
Brustein put it, "Clinton has undoubtedly emerged as the most popular
actor in America, even if Republican legislators keep walking out on his
act."[34]

Of course, an ideological battle is on, too. The fact is that political
commentary gets played out at the cinema, and films like *Primary Colors*
and *The Contender* are weighing in on Clinton's legacy. After all, just
as pundits and journalists wish to weigh in, so, too, do screenwriters and
directors. In the summer of 2000, Joe Eszterhas, the author of such films
as *Basic Instinct* and *Jagged Edge*, published an "odd, mutant" book
(fiction and nonfiction) called *American Rhapsody*. In it, Eszterhas gave
his own judgmental version of the Lewinsky scandal and impeachment
hearings, along with a withering, sarcastic assessment of Clinton's role.
Eszterhas said he felt compelled to write about the political saga after
following it closely on TV, particularly after watching the president's
denials: "What I cared very much about was when he jabbed his finger
in my face . . . almost as though he were a guy in a bar who'd been
challenged, and said, 'I did not have sexual relations with that woman,
Miss Lewinsky.' "[35] Among Eszterhas's unique artistic devices: the nar-
rative perspective provided by the president's penis. Fantastic or not,
fictional or not, such assessments of the Clinton era began pouring out
in 1999 and 2000, as Americans tried to make sense of the man who
had become the last president of the twentieth century. And as we'll see
in the next chapter, the war over the meaning of that legacy has only
just started.

NOTES

1. Thomas Rosteck, "The Intertextuality of 'The Man From Hope': Bill
Clinton as Person, as Persona, as Star?" in *Bill Clinton on Stump, State, and*

Stage: The Rhetorical Road to the White House, ed. Stephen A. Smith (Fayetteville: University of Arkansas Press, 1994), p. 225.

2. Richard D. Wilkins, " 'Dissed Colors,' " *Business Journal* (October 28, 1996), p. 25.

3. Donald Foster, "Primary Culprit," *New York* (February 26, 1996), pp. 50–57. Also see Foster, *Author Unknown: On the Trail of Anonymous* (New York: Henry Holt, 1996), pp. 53–95.

4. Donald Foster, *Author Unknown*, p. 80.

5. Joe Klein, quoted in Staci D. Kramer, "Primary Colors Timeline," *Quill* 84 (September 1996), p. 9.

6. Mark Miller, "Who Wrote the Book on Bill?" *Newsweek* (January 26, 1996), p. 29.

7. Kenneth Turan, *Los Angeles Times* (March 20, 1998), p. F1.

8. Anonymous, *Primary Colors: A Novel of Politics* (New York: Random House, 1996), p. 3.

9. Michael P. Shea, *Boston Globe* (June 4, 2000), p. H2.

10. Ibid.

11. John Travolta, quoted by Richard L. Eldredge, *Atlanta Journal and Constitution* (May 14, 1998), p. D2.

12. Turan, p. F1.

13. James Carville, quoted by Warren St. John, *London Guardian* (March 13, 1997), p. T2.

14. Mark Miller, "Who Wrote the Book on Bill?" p. 29.

15. For further examination of this issue, see Ellen Alderman and Caroline Kennedy, "Can a Journalist's Novel Be Libelous?" *Columbia Journalism Review* 36 (July/August 1997), p. 55.

16. Mike Nichols, quoted in Jeffrey Wells, "No Sex, Please, We're American," *People* 49 (February 16, 1998), p. 20.

17. Jonathan Freedland, *New Statesman* (March 13, 1998), p. 47.

18. Thelma Adams, *New York Post* (December 26, 1997), p. 41.

19. Barbara Wickens, "Hollywood or Washington?" *Maclean's* (February 9, 1998), p. 14.

20. "Notebook," *Time* (February 2, 1998), p. 16.

21. Barry Levinson, "Hey, We Were Just Kidding," *Newsweek* (February 9, 1998), p. 51.

22. Andrew T. Olivastro, "Sex, Lies, and Videotape," *World & I* (November 1998), p. 54.

23. Editorial, *USA Today* (January 27, 1998), p. A13.

24. Justin Brown, "Why Serb Chief Whips Up Anti-U.S. Fervor," *Christian Science Monitor* (April 1, 1999), p. 1.

25. Christopher Hitchens, *No One Left to Lie to: The Triangulations of William Jefferson Clinton* (London: Verso, 1999), pp. 87–103.

26. Paul Burgess, "Hawkeye Pierce to Patton—Clinton's Knack for the Quick Change," Knight-Ridder/Tribune News Service (June 21, 1999).

27. John Simon, "Improprieties," *National Review* (October 23, 2000), p. 86.

28. Part of the reason? Writer and co-producer Lawrence O'Donnell, who had recently worked for Senator Daniel Patrick Moynihan and sometimes appeared as a pundit on MSNBC. According to O'Donnell, "Politics has become show biz." Quoted in Howard Kurtz, "Leaving Wonkville, Entering Punditville," *Washington Post* (August 21, 2000), p. C1.

29. Rod Lurie, quoted in "Hollywood Inspired by Clinton Era," *Milwaukee Journal* (November 4, 2000), p. B6.

30. Terrence Rafferty, "Holiday Films: When Hollywood Puts Its Spin on the Oval Office," *New York Times* (November 5, 2000), p. 2.

31. Jonathan Freedland, *New Statesman* (March 13, 1998), p. 47.

32. For discussion about this journalistic controversy, see Howard Kurtz, "Anna and the Kings of Spin," *Washington Post* (October 16, 2000), p. C1.

33. Richard Reeves, "No Movie Can Capture Clinton Character," *Buffalo News* (March 31, 1998), p. B3.

34. Robert Brustein, "An Oscar for Clinton," *New Republic* (March 8, 1999), p. 31.

35. Joe Eszterhas, quoted in Robert W. Welkos, "Eszterhas Starts a New Chapter," *Los Angeles Times* (July 18, 2000).

7

Legacy: "The Final Election"

INTRODUCTION

Journalists seldom express much desire to talk about the historical impact of a one-term president. The press seems to treat such officeholders as the forgettable blips between strong executives. A two-term president is another matter. And an incumbent who was impeached, of course, naturally warrants more historical reflection. Not long after being reelected in 1996, in fact, Bill Clinton's potential legacy was already the subject of increased rumination in the popular press. How would future generations judge the first Democratic president to win a second term since Franklin Roosevelt? Members of the mass media have been chewing on that question for the last several years, and not surprisingly there's very little consensus as to the answer. One pattern that is noticeable, however, is an increased tendency since 1999 to emphasize Clinton's impact, to deem him either very bad or very good, but nonetheless to value his significance. Clinton's impeachment obviously had much to do with that tendency. Since Senate trials of a president are rare, they necessarily inflate the importance of those on trial. Would we otherwise remember Andrew Johnson for anything other than succeeding Abraham Lincoln?

Yet, Clinton's presidency was particularly stormy, filled with unusual acrimony and confrontation, regularly beset with controversy, and often adrift in uncharted waters. "[H]is tenure in the end," one NBC correspondent said, "would be marked by a tumultuous pattern of success, failure and scandal."[1] According to TV host Geraldo Rivera, President Clinton led the public down an emotionally exhausting trail: "At various times . . . he inspired us, he appalled us, he delighted us, he duped us, he also, often, surprised us."[2] Though he lamented more than once to friends that his White House years never coincided with a monumental challenge such as war or depression, Bill Clinton *did* serve in interesting times—and for which he himself was largely to blame. "Indeed," writes the *Los Angeles Times*, "he is widely seen as a tragic figure whose gargantuan personal weaknesses denied him the greatness that his political genius seemed to promise."[3] As former adviser David Gergen put it, Clinton has shown himself abler than just about any other politician to get out of a jam, but also more likely than other politicians to get *into* a jam.[4]

In the following pages, I will look at popular commentary concerning President Clinton's legacy. For convenience's sake, I have organized this examination into two chronological sections: preimpeachment opinion from approximately 1996 to late 1998, and postimpeachment opinion from 1999 to 2001. (For commentary during the impeachment period, see chapter 5.) Much of this commentary is divided, uncertain, and oftentimes rather heated. It is also quite diverse, ranging from the *National Review*'s "A Farewell to the Big Creep" cover story to the *New Yorker*'s "Bill Clinton Looks Back," a cover story with an artist's sketch of the president riding off into the sunset.[5] Most observers, however sympathetic, recognized that the Clinton presidency was darkly tainted. At the same time, most observers, however critical, conceded the buoyancy in Clinton's White House years. Was the spin master getting to even his harshest critics?

PREIMPEACHMENT (1996–1998)

Assessments about Bill Clinton in the two years following the 1996 election were bland blends of praise for his political instincts mixed with criticism for his political instincts. No one doubted that the baby-boomer president was tough, smart, hardworking, and resilient. But his reputation was also that of a politically timid compromiser. He avoided confrontational stands on principle, preferring to join the most moderate position on an issue. The one exception to this rule came during the government shutdowns of 1995 and 1996, when the president effectively called the Republicans' bluff. In those episodes, it was Newt Gingrich who "blinked first," the GOP which underestimated Clinton's resolve. "His backbone was stiffer than they anticipated," Health and Human Services Secretary Donna Shalala remembered.[6] Such instances were rare, though, and Clinton regularly displeased both liberals and conservatives.

In the fall of 1998, a *Nation* round table devoted to the significance of Clinton's two terms sounded extremely gloomy. "The first cold-war presidency could never find its point," ex-Labor Secretary Robert Reich said. "Bill Clinton occasionally tried to tell us, but he wasn't bold enough or consistent enough; he seemed to compromise and weasel too much, and thus America never trusted him enough."[7] Rogers M. Smith called Clinton "more Nero than hero," a political leader with little courage or conviction. "His legacy is that whenever it came time to stand apart and summon Americans to resist their baser impulses, he chose instead to plunge into the crowd at the rope line, seeking all-too-familiar hugs."[8] Barbara Ehrenreich commented wryly that Clinton had pioneered only in oral sex. Ronald Steel, analyzing Clinton's agenda overseas, concludes that the president's foreign policy has been almost indistinguishable from his trade policy. "What Clinton will be best remembered for (dalliances aside) is NAFTA and the World Trade Organization. This is the legacy of a technocrat and coordinator, not an innovator."[9] Jonathan Schell credited Clinton for his courageous support of deficit reduction and the first budget bill. Sean Wilentz praised him for having "restored American political centrism," for being "a moderating force during the nation's second Gilded Age."[10] Overall, however, this liberal round table expressed disappointment and frustration.

Part of these commentators' problem with Clinton was that he had not been courageous enough regarding policy, had not been sufficiently liberal or progressive, but instead gravitated too readily toward compromise and toward the center. "In his first term, he progressed from bold ideas such as national health insurance to bite-size ones such as school uniforms," the *Milwaukee Journal-Sentinel* observed.[11] Not long after reelection, many in the Democratic Party, such as Representative Richard Gephardt of Missouri, were questioning Clinton's strategy, fearful that the president's ambition to make history by appeasing Republicans and reducing the deficit would hurt their political base.[12] A Cornell professor, writing in the *Los Angeles Times* midway through Clinton's second term, concluded that "the only legacy I can identify is his contribution to his own party, by pulling it to the right, making it a 'Yes, but' version of the other party."[13] Some writers even accused Clinton of outright moral bankruptcy. Michael Kelly of the *Washington Post* charged that the Democratic Party's campaign-finance abuse (President Clinton's fundraisers in particular) before and during 1996 had "utterly destroyed the old liberal-moralist position. . . . There will only be Clintonism, which is the philosophy that money talks without the honesty to admit itself."[14]

Another aspect of their disenchantment, though, was the president's inability to avoid distracting personal scandals. Even a year before his impeachment, one quarter of people over sixty and three-quarters of those under thirty already thought Clinton would be remembered mainly for his private peccadilloes.[15] In a CNN round table from 1997, correspondent Charles Bierbauer marvelled at the administration's penchant for a "tabloid presidency," for the tendency to make "both good news and bad news at the same time."[16] That TV discussion resulted from a U.S. Supreme Court decision late that spring affirming Paula Jones's right to continue her lawsuit against the president while he was in office. "One hundred years from today," political analyst Martin Walker said on the program, "5th and 6th graders will be learning in their constitutional law books . . . of a case called *Jones vs. Clinton*, which established the important principle that nobody, including the president, is above the law." On the question of history's ultimate judgment, in fact, David Gergen argued that such scandals might eventually take a toll on the Clinton presidency:

[T]hese allegations—these controversies that have dogged him . . . like a tin can tied to the Clinton presidency . . . make a lot of clatter, but whether they will seriously trip him up or not, I think, remains to be seen. So far, I don't think it's had much damage on his standing with the public. I do think these kind of allegations—the fact [that] this case goes forward, will damage his standing with historians, and after all, that's the final election that he's running for; how he will wind up with the historians.[17]

Gergen's comments came seven months before the Monica Lewinsky story first broke. Within the space of a few years, Clinton's "final election" would seem headed for disaster.

POSTIMPEACHMENT (1999–2001)

Issues

How was President Clinton remembered during his last few years in office? The testimony varies depending on the issue. Few writers gush over the Clinton years. On the subject of civil liberties, the president has received atrocious reviews. Liberals have castigated him for his record on issues touching the First, Third, and Fourth Amendments, and people like the writer Christopher Hitchens and law professor Alan Dershowitz have shaken their heads in disbelief at the record Clinton leaves behind.[18] On defense and national security issues, his legacy is scarcely better, with low military morale a touchy political issue in both 1996 and 2000, and with critical breaches in nuclear missile technology the stuff of at least one major scandal. Worse, the president's ties to Chinese campaign donors eroded his credibility on Sino-American relations and threatened, for a short time, to trigger another investigation. William Safire, the columnist Bill Clinton once threatened to punch in the nose, has been the president's toughest foreign policy critic. He believes it is this "Asian connection," the connection between Indonesian lobbyist James Riady and the Democratic Party, for which Clinton has most to be ashamed.[19]

A more mixed assessment comes on such matters as his contributions to the lives of American blacks and other ethnic minorities. Debra Mathis, White House correspondent for Gannett news service, concluded that while some results were directly "attributable only to him and his activism . . . some of it was coincidental" and would have come about "no matter who had been in the White House."[20] A Harvard University study nonetheless found overwhelming approval among blacks (77%) of Clinton's performance. Almost nine in ten rated him an above-average president.[21] Leaders within the civil rights establishment have also given Clinton high marks, much of it based on personal experience around the president. Congressman John Lewis of Georgia and National Association for the Advancement of Colored People (NAACP) chairman Julian Bond both say that Clinton always "fit in" with black audiences, seemed natural and at ease, and appeared to be one with them, spiritually and emotionally, if not one of them. Novelist Toni Morrison, after all, once dubbed Bill Clinton America's "first black president." "He's got the culture down; it's not phony," says Roger Wilkins, before adding, "But sometimes his racial program was lousy."[22]

The economy is probably the most frequently cited benefit of the Clinton years. No one says that it was all Clinton's doing, of course, and many pundits challenge whether the president had very much at all to do with it. But a substantial body of opinion contends that without Clinton's determination to bring about deficit reduction in his first term, the leaps and bounds of the American economy in the second term would not have happened. In his last State of the Union address before the nation, President Clinton summarized the country's prosperity:

We began the new century with over 20 million new jobs, the fastest economic growth in more than 30 years, the lowest unemployment rates in 30 years, the lowest poverty rates in 20 years, the lowest African-American and Hispanic unemployment rates on record, the first back-to-back surpluses in 42 years. And next month, America will achieve the longest period of economic growth in our entire history.[23]

Was he personally to thank for this astonishing boom? To some extent, yes. He was committed to deficit reduction and receptive to welfare reform, and he supported liberal trade policies and global integration. Someday, in fact, historians may give him more credit for his contributions to the world economy than the American economy.[24] At home, though, he accepted the need for fiscal discipline and worked well with Federal Reserve Chairman Alan Greenspan. He does deserve some praise, then. However, as National Public Radio economic correspondent John Ydstie says, "a big share of the credit for the prosperous times should go elsewhere. After all, Mr. Clinton was fortunate to be in the White House at a time of savvy monetary policy under Alan Greenspan, at a time when American companies were stronger than ever and during the flowering of computer technology, which boosted the productivity of American workers."[25] Clinton helped, in other words, but he was barely more integral to the boom of the 1990s than President Harding had been to that of the 1920s. "Quite honestly," concludes the *St. Louis Post-Dispatch*, "the country would probably have been as prosperous with George Bush in the White House as Bill Clinton."[26]

Moreover, some critics, such as Stephen Moore of the conservative Cato Institute, go further and contend that America "survived" Clinton's early efforts and that Republicans "saved" the president from himself.[27] John Kasich, a former Republican congressman from Ohio, who negotiated the final budget agreement with the White House, insists that without his party's determination, a balanced budget would never have come about: "No way in the world would that have happened."[28] Kasich says that a Congress controlled by Democrats, as in Clinton's first two years, would never have supported such legislation. Valid as many of their arguments are, though, Moore and Kasich underestimate Clinton's mastery of, affinity for, and pragmatic approach to complicated economic issues. He had won the presidency largely because of his swaggering command of economic policy, and he was perfectly prepared to compromise on a great many things to restore America's fiscal health. None-theless, Moore and Kasich's judgments ring truer than those of Clinton's defenders. Robert Litan, an Office of Management and Budget official in the Clinton administration, for one, concedes that deficit reduction hinged on Republican support. And the North American Free Trade Agreement (NAFTA) and welfare reform, says another writer, "were really Republican initiatives [Clinton] ultimately endorsed."[29] Certainly, America's 42nd president was one of its most economically astute pres-idents, but he was also the indisputable beneficiary of some plain good luck. And luck does not automatically translate into legacy: "He was blessed but somewhat limited by the robust economy. In a time of pros-perity, a president has few opportunities for the bold stroke—fewer com-pelling problems to solve."[30] "Mr. Clinton was a lucky president," concluded the *Pittsburgh Post-Gazette*.[31]

The other area Clinton has received considerable credit for is the en-vironment. Most of the praise, though, came at the end of his second term. During most of his presidency, Clinton amassed a mixed record. In 1997, for example, he pushed for stricter measures on soot and smog, but passed on tougher international standards for gas emissions. National Public Radio's Daniel Schorr described the contrast:

It did look funny when one day President Clinton has been put into a rather no escape position by EPA administrator Carol Browner and by Vice President Al Gore. And so he comes out and he manages to override a lot of his own advisers. And he endorses tough new standards on soot and smog. Then, now being hailed as poster boy for the environment, next day he goes up [to the] United Nations and says "nyet" to setting targets for reducing . . . greenhouse gases—the ones that cause global warming. That leaves the environmental summit to close, and a big attitude of doom.[32]

As his last term began to wind down, Clinton sought to make up for lost ground and actually appeared to be gunning for Teddy Roosevelt's land conservation record. Roosevelt invoked the Antiquities Act eighteen times. In the year 2000 alone, Clinton used it a dozen times, setting aside a third of the country's land under federally protected status.[33]

Politics after Clinton

An important Clinton legacy has been his influence on politics. His political style, above all, has set a new benchmark for how to get elected and how to govern. "He has personalized the presidency," one scholar

has said,[34] but Clinton has just as clearly helped to personalize electioneering in general. Mara Liasson, who covered the White House for National Public Radio, explains:

I think he's definitely set a new standard for campaigning. I think it's a standard
that neither George Bush or Al Gore came close to in this election [of 2000],
but he was the most talented retail politician of his generation. . . . I think now
it's almost a requirement that candidates hold town meetings, that they show
that they can relate to ordinary people, that there's a certain amount of intimacy
that they have to show with voters now with a stop on "The Oprah Show" or
the "Regis" show is required. And I think President Clinton really started all of
that.[35]

The soft, informal approach permanently influenced other campaigns
since Clinton's initial run. "It's no longer enough for candidates on the
campaign trail simply to deliver the goods," one Washington correspondent noted in 2000. "They have to be able to deliver a punch line as
well."[36]

Some commentators have argued that what Bill Clinton has done is
to have "feminized" American politics, to have changed not just the
tactics but the tone and emphasis:

Throughout his presidency, Clinton has constantly displayed a kind of feminine
style; focusing on domestic affairs more than foreign and military ones, per-
fecting the Oprah-like "I feel your pain" style of politics, creating an agenda
centered on small, specific improvements such as family leave rather than over-
arching themes. . . . After all, the most celebrated moment of both conventions
this year wasn't a speech or a demonstration, but a kiss.[37]

Although I would challenge these observers' use of the term "feminize,"
I believe they are correct in the types of changes they describe. There is
more stress on harmony, on pleasantness to the point of inanity, on per-
sonability, on informality.

The permanent campaign, alternative mass media, war-room tactics,
the emphasis on empathy, genuine and indefatigable charm offensives,
the never-say-die attitude—these have been the tools with which Clinton
has succeeded and which others have tried to emulate. Much of Clinton's
personal political brilliance actually stems from simple, time-honored
precepts: a capacity to learn and adapt; "his ability to win friends";[38] and
a remarkable resiliency. According to former Republican senator Warren

Rudman of New Hampshire, "He's the toughest person on the inside that I've known. . . . He's just powerful, powerful."[39]

Clinton's personal fortitude is so celebrated that some political scientists have described his political style as a combination of seducer and survivor—someone who indulges certain risky behaviors but thrives on the challenge of overcoming censure when he's caught. "Throughout his public life," one such scholar has concluded, "Clinton has repeated the cycle of excess, rejection, perseverance, and, ultimately, rejuvenation."[40]

His impact on his own party is a curious one. Bill Clinton put the Democratic Party through some unusual paces, refurbishing its image yet oftentimes injuring specific candidates. He divided the party between "old" Democrats and "new,"[41] causing friction between those who advocated a liberal, progressive course and those who favored a centrist agenda. Of the latter, Dick Morris, for example, has maintained that the president's centrism "ultimately saved the Democratic party from itself" by keeping its members more in touch with the thinking of average Americans and therefore more viable at the voting booth.[42] Other observers have been quick to challenge that notion, however. "In all essentials, the Clinton-Gore administration has been Republican, and not all that moderate," writes Christopher Hitchens.[43] Some critics were more charitable, yet still uneasy with Clinton's sinuous policy turns. Credited with restoring Democrats' credibility, with making them "competitive again on the presidential level," Clinton also hurt the party at the polls— in 1994, in 1996, and again, in 2000.[44] By the end of his second term, Republicans had recaptured many state legislatures, governorships, the House of Representatives, and precisely half the Senate.

Moreover, the circumstances that led to his impeachment hurt him by unavoidably eroding his political capital in the party. This was clear during his last year in office, when he sometimes resembled a likeable leper. George Watson, of ABC News, said in October that "Clinton's greatest legacy would be the election of his vice president to succeed him. But Gore is resisting Clinton's embrace."[45] Indeed, one of Clinton's most interesting political influences in the late 1990s was the distance to which many major Democratic office seekers in 2000 quietly disassociated themselves from him. The president "was kept out of state after state, usually at the insistence of the Gore campaign, but sometimes at the insistence of local candidates as well. He was simply too hot."[46] Gore bent over backward not to include Clinton in campaign appearances, not to mention his name in speeches, even to offer a gentle rebuke of the president with a few cautious words and with his choice of a vice presidential running mate, Joe Lieberman, the Democratic senator most critical of Clinton during impeachment. Polls confirmed sharply conflicting opinion over the president, which is probably why in a campaign year Democrats often preferred not to invoke his name, while Republicans positively wallowed in it. Certainly, some wanted Gore to lose as a lesson for Clinton and his party. Said William Safire, "I have a heavy case of Clinton fatigue, and know that shameless fellow would interpret a Gore victory as the nation's apology to him."[47] So, the politician whose centrism had been credited with "saving the Democratic Party" in the 1990s was mainly ostracized as a political liability in the 2000 presidential campaign.[48]

Friends and Foes

Virtually all Clinton's defenders—even former staff members—agree that the president's personal weaknesses badly hurt his eight years in office. While they accord him more credit for various accomplishments and conclude he did a reasonably good job, they also lament the missed opportunities, the waste, the distraction, the carelessness, the timidity and "small-bore agenda."[49] Many of them feel cheated by a president who did not turn out to be as magnificent as they had hoped. "For most committed Americans on the left," Michael Kazin writes, "the administration has been, at best, a disappointment."[50] "I was one of those who wanted to believe he was more liberal than he was," confesses historian Doris Kearns Goodwin, "But I admit there was hardly any evidence of it, even when he was freed up at times."[51]

Clinton's rank-and-file supporters usually emphasize the president's smarts. Movie mogul Harvey Weinstein was impressed with the way he could talk to him about films, discuss the economy with economists, and make obscure music references to someone like David Geffen. He says flatly that Bill Clinton is "the most intelligent person I've ever met."[52] His magnetism was also legendary—"rakish charm on overload," a "master" of American politics.[53] Clinton developed a reputation as someone whom even political opponents came to like. His unceasing amiability stemmed from his fabled ability to relate with common people, to talk to anyone, to make pleasant chitchat even when he'd had no sleep the night before. Bill Clinton was both the ultimate social creature and the quintessential political animal.

How do his fiercest critics remember Clinton? More than anything, it seems, they single out the moral failings, the personal flaws, the cloudy ethics—all of which did arguably erode the credibility and integrity of the Oval Office during the 1990s. "I think he's an insanitary guy.... I think he degraded the presidency," said Christopher Hitchens, perhaps Clinton's most trenchant as well as dogged critic.[54] Television comedian Dennis Miller said he had been invited to White House dinners but couldn't bring himself to go: "I just don't respect him."[55] And even while the American people consistently valued Bill Clinton's job performance, they just as consistently thought him a liar all the while. In addition to the dishonesty ("I didn't dodge the draft"; "I didn't inhale"), critics complained about his unprincipled craving for popularity, his overreliance on public opinion polls, a lack of dignity and respect for the office (a charge aimed at Democrats for more than a century and a half, to be sure, but aggravated by what columnist Gail Collins called a "sleazy exit from Washington"),[56] instances of sexual impropriety, and, most seriously, appearances of corruption—whether involving campaign finance abuses or midnight pardons for political friends. "He was unlucky in only one respect: His own worst enemy was himself."[57] Robert Bartley, editor of the *Wall Street Journal*, writes that for him it was former Associate Attorney General Webb Hubbell's resignation that clinched his worst fears: "We always had suspicions that Clinton was corrupt, but I have to say I was surprised by the extent, or the brazenness, of it."[58]

The increasingly suspicious *New York Times* took Clinton to task in January 2001 for his last-minute pardon of fugitive financier Marc Rich and others, saying the president had abused the pardoning process and allowed politics, rather than legal merit to influence his judgment.[59] In fact, the *Times* went on something of an editorial rampage against the ex-president for the pardons, calling them "[m]ore controversial than any since Gerald Ford bestowed official forgiveness on Richard Nixon" (January 29), "shockingly indefensible" (February 1), and a "self-destructive attack on his own legacy" (February 23).[60] The editorial described how Clinton blamed Republicans and the media for his problems but, in any case, usually forced the country to choose between tolerating "outrageous" behavior and taking burdensome legal action. If the president was concerned about his legacy, criticisms like these indicate he may have permanently sabotaged it. As one scholar summarized the persistent volume of condemnation, "President Clinton has been the poster boy for defective character in the 1990s."[61]

Other Presidents

In December 2000, Gallup polled Americans to survey their views of the Clinton presidency. On personal marks, the president scored badly, as the public found him increasingly dishonest, and most people (74%) thought his two terms would be remembered for sex scandals and impeachment, not his job approval ratings. Yet, overall, during his two terms, President Clinton scored about average (55%) in the public's approval of his job performance, and 65% during 2000 alone, which is the highest figure for any president in his final year.[62] Most telling of all, though, is that just one month after the House of Representatives impeached him, a staggering number of Americans (81%) said they personally would rate Clinton's presidency a success.[63]

On December 31, 2000, Arthur Schlesinger, Jr., told George Will in an interview on ABC's Sunday program, *This Week*, that he still believed Clinton ranked as a "high average" among American presidents.[64] Historians James MacGregor Burns and Georgia Sorenson are tougher on Clinton, saying he failed to overcome opposition and instead continually caved.[65] Historian David Kennedy compares Clinton to Grover Cleveland, both of whom "announced grand schemes but accomplished little." Indeed, according to Kennedy, the events leading up to Clinton's impeachment "were but the last and redundant nails in the coffin of the Clinton presidency. He has been effectively a crippled duck almost from the outset and for reasons that Grover Cleveland would have understood: political paralysis and the inability of either party to build a stable electoral majority."[66]

Sean Wilentz has also invoked the Cleveland comparison, saying of both men that they were probably the "ablest" candidates elected in the last third of their respective centuries.[67] "Gilded-age executive" hardly stands as a glowing testimonial. And the gilded label carries a pejorative connotation, the insinuation that one is superficial, glib, and crass—or else has merely risen just enough above the superficial, the glib, and the crass to stand out. As a respondent to an *Arizona Republic* survey said, "Bill Clinton will . . . be remembered as silver-tongued—a man who could spin the truth to this advantage and captivate his audience with promises he would never fulfill. That will be his legacy."[68] Certainly, Clinton etched a vivid and memorable presidency. As a newspaper reader wrote to his editor, "I heard a man who opposed Clinton's presidency say he read six books about him. The next president will be a veritable stranger."[69]

Bill Clinton has sometimes been compared to Richard Nixon, though it is not a comparison normally favored by either stalwart Democrats or resolute Republicans. "Not since Richard Nixon has there been a president who has inspired so much cynicism about politics and politicians in general," writes Pulitzer prize-winning editor Paul Greenberg. "More and more, Bill Clinton comes to resemble a Richard Nixon with bonhomie."[70] Christopher Hitchens agrees: Because of Clinton, "American Democratic liberalism has lost its honor and prestige and has proved itself as adept in making excuses for power as any Babbitt in the Nixon era."[71] Commentators who invoke the name of Nixon do so because he, too, was smart, was thought of as dishonest, and would have surely faced impeachment had he not resigned. What is more, regardless of his trip to China or the war in Vietnam or Russo-American relations, we remember him first for resigning over the Watergate fiasco.[72] Some writers even contend that Nixon comes off better in the comparison. Ohio State University historian Joan Hoff says Nixon at least fought for what he believed in: "He took risks, he had some success. But what does Bill Clinton stand for? He has no strong inner compass, he wavers a lot, and that's not much to build a legacy on."[73]

Journalists' comparisons have proved more generous. Many pundits put Clinton alongside such exemplary political retailers as Lyndon Johnson and Franklin Roosevelt. Former CBS White House correspondent Mark Knoller calls Clinton "perhaps the most masterful politician since FDR, if not including FDR."[74] The "most gifted U.S. politician in a half century," says Texas journalist Michael Hedges.[75] According to the *Los Angeles Times*, "friend and foe alike consider him the most gifted politician of his age."[76] David Gergen speculated on NBC's *Meet the Press* that Clinton will in posterity fare a bit like John F. Kennedy: "well-remembered by the public, not as well-remembered by historians."[77] Gergen did underscore Clinton's numerous intellectual gifts and the historical context for his abilities and disposition:

[T]his was an enormously talented man, one of the most talented people we've had in the Oval Office in the last 100 years, and gifted in so many ways. And he had a passion for change and for improving people's lives, and using the government as a vehicle to do that. I think he was one of the last of the presidents who will probably believe as strongly as he did in that. And a great number of people in the lower end of the spectrum felt that connection with him, and that's why you find, particularly in the black community, this sense that Bill Clinton was the best president they had since Franklin Roosevelt.[78]

Part of the problem, of course, is the lack of some distinguishing legislation that can be associated with Clinton. As Douglas Brinkley has pointed out, FDR had the New Deal, Truman the national security apparatus, Eisenhower the interstate highway system, and Johnson the Civil Rights Act. "There really isn't something like that during Bill Clinton's eight years."[79] Indeed, most commentators look at 1998–1999 as a period when much might have been accomplished but wasn't because of the scandals besetting the White House. Stanford historian Terry Moe says that Clinton had a "unique" opportunity to address major challenges, yet failed to do so. "In the end, he hasn't accomplished all that much, and I think that is how history should judge him."[80] One newspaper simply offered this epitaph: "Bill Clinton, the president who might have been great."[81]

CONCLUSION

Why so much fuss about Clinton's legacy? Is it routine historical arm-chairing, or something else? Something within Bill Clinton? Has President Clinton been "simply more obsessed with the issue than his predecessors?"[82] I think he probably has. And the reasons are not difficult to surmise. As one of only two presidents ever to be impeached, William Jefferson Clinton wants to be remembered for something other than that sad piece of American history, which is probably why he wrote more than 30,000 pages of new regulations in eleventh-hour executive decisions; why he tried, only at the end of his presidency, to recharge his relationship with ordinary journalists and press associations; why he had, perhaps above all, labored so tirelessly to broker a peace agreement in the Middle East. Such a foreign policy coup might have gone a long way toward overshadowing his legal and ethical failings at home, toward filling Bill Clinton's postimpeachment "need for redemption."[83] So, even though the president has at times (during bad times especially) accused the media of being consumed with the legacy question, there seems little doubt that he himself was often preoccupied with it. According to Brookings Institute president Michael Armacost, "One of the defining characteristics of Mr. Clinton's legacy may be the self-consciousness of its pursuit."[84] "No past president would so publicly fondle his 'legacy,' " says conservative columnist R. Emmett Tyrrell, Jr.[85] And that preoccupation may not bode well for the future. Former Republican strategist Ed Rollins notes that he has "always found presidents who worry about the historian's role and their legacy aren't very good presidents."[86]

Yet, there is more to William Jefferson Clinton than just the defensive reflexes of a desperate politician anxious to restore his tarnished reputation. First of all, he has always shown a keen interest in U.S. history, has carefully studied past presidencies, and is an avid reader of presidential biographies. More than just his fascination with the American past, though, there is a strong personal and philosophical disposition. Since he was a young man, the ambitious Arkansan dreamed of being president and of making a difference in the lives of others. Like the heroes of his youth, John F. Kennedy and Martin Luther King, Jr., Bill Clinton channelled all his energies, talents, and charms into the realm of public service. From mastering intricate policy controversies to joking with voters on the campaign trail, he has always revelled in the American political process and believed in its ability to deliver what people want. "As one of the few presidents with authentically humble roots," a newspaper editor pointed out, "Mr. Clinton truly believes that government should help people."[87] He is himself possessed by a "passionate desire to do good."[88]

President Clinton will try to leave behind a positive legacy, in part because that is why he ran for public office in the first place and why he has been doing it ever since. William Safire's charge that the president was "frantically scrambling to patch together his claim to a legacy" bears some truth, but only if you consider that Bill Clinton cared deeply about a legacy even before he was sworn in on January 20, 1993.[89] Finally, it should be noted that Bill Clinton left office still a young man at fifty-four. There is, perhaps, a good bit more legacy yet to come. As for his White House years, comparisons to subsequent presidents will likely put his stint in office into sharper relief.

NOTES

1. Claire Shipman, NBC News, *Today* (January 19, 2001).

2. Geraldo Rivera, CNBC, *Rivera Live*, "Clinton Legacy" (January 16, 2001).

3. Richard T. Cooper and Jack Nelson, "The 'Natural' Wraps Up His 8-Year Run," *Los Angeles Times* (January 14, 2001), p. A1.

4. David Gergen, quoted in PBS, *Frontline*, "The Clinton Years" (January 16, 2001).

5. "A Farewell to the Big Creep," *National Review* (November 20, 2000); "Bill Clinton Looks Back," *New Yorker* (October 16–23, 2000). In a special survey, the *Arizona Republic* concluded that the "views were fairly evenly split." "Last Week We Asked: How Will Clinton's Presidency Be Recalled?" *Arizona Republic* (August 26, 2000), p. B6.

6. Donna Shalala, interview with Chris Bury, ABC News, *Nightline*, "The Clinton Years"; broadcast on ABC News, *This Week* (January 7, 2001). "The

budget bill was that rare thing in his career, an act of real political courage,"
Jonathan Schell wrote. Schell, "Beyond Monica: The Future of Clinton's Past,"
The Nation 267 (September 7, 1998), p. 13.

7. Schell, "Beyond Monica: The Future of Clinton's Past," *The Nation* 267
(September 7, 1998), p. 11.

8. Rogers M. Smith, in ibid.

9. Ronald Steel, in ibid.

10. Sean Wilentz, in ibid.

11. Craig Gilbert, "Clinton's Legacy Begins to Form," *Milwaukee Journal-Sentinel* (January 16, 1997), p. 2.

12. Associated Press, "Clinton's Legacy Plans Get in Democrats' Way," *St.
Louis Post-Dispatch* (July 8, 1997), p. A4.

13. Theodore J. Lowi, "Why Clinton Must Demand Impeachment," *Los Angeles Times* (August 14, 1998), p. B9. See also Michael Meeropal, *Surrender:
How the Clinton Administration Completed the Reagan Revolution* (Ann Arbor:
University of Michigan Press, 1998), pp. 242–64.

14. Michael Kelly, "Clinton's Legacy," *Washington Post* (October 30, 1997),
p. A23.

15. Claudia Deane and Ruth Marcus, "Generations Split on Clinton Legacy,"
Washington Post (February 8, 1998), p. A19.

16. Charles Bierbauer, CNN, *Inside Politics* (May 28, 1997).

17. David Gergen, interview, ibid.

18. See, for example, Christopher Hitchens, "Bill of Goods?" *Mother Jones*
25 (September/October 2000), p. 55; Alan M. Dershowitz, *Sexual McCarthyism:
Clinton, Starr, and the Emerging Constitutional Crisis* (New York: Basic Books,
1998), pp. 149–161; Stuart Taylor, Jr., "How Liberals Got Tired of the Freedom
of Speech," *National Journal* (October 14, 2000).

19. "An American president's foreign policy decisions were substantially influenced by unlawful campaign contributions at critical times from a foreign
source. In my view, that inescapable judgment will be more damning in history's
eyes than Whitewater cover-ups or any abuses for which Clinton was impeached." William Safire, "Riady Cops a Plea," *New York Times* (January 15,
2001), p. A19.

20. Debra Mathis, quoted in CNN, *Both Sides with Jesse Jackson*, "What
Will Clinton's Legacy Be Among African-Americans?" (January 15, 2001).

21. By contrast, fewer than five out of ten white persons rated Clinton an
above-average president. Cited in Michael Hedges, "The Clinton Years: Legacy
Viewed as Mixed," *Houston Chronicle* (January 14, 2001), p. A1.

22. Roger Wilkins, "What We'll Remember," *Time* 156 (November 20,
2000), p. 90.

23. Clinton, State of the Union Address, January 2000.

24. "[T]he Clinton administration was even more nimble in managing global
economic issues. Recognizing the growing significance of a global economy,

Clinton encouraged free trade, risking the anger of a Democrat's allies in Big Labor. He pushed through Congress a controversial bailout of the Mexican peso, averting a massive financial meltdown. And believing that democratic reforms will follow economic growth, he also secured Most Favored Nation trading status for China." Editorial, "History Will View Clinton Legacy Favorably," *Atlanta Constitution* (January 19, 2001), p. A22.

25. John Ydstie, National Public Radio, *Morning Edition*, "Economic Legacy of President Bill Clinton" (January 12, 2001). Peter Edleman, formerly the assistant secretary of Health and Human Services, offers another perspective. Edleman argues that Clinton "helped some a little and . . . hurt others a lot." Whom did he hurt? Poor people, according to Edleman: "The poor, on average, are a little better off, but the wealthy are in clover up to their eyeballs." Peter Edleman, "President Clinton Hurt Poor People More than Helping Them When He Signed the 1996 Welfare Reform Law," National Public Radio, *Morning Edition* (January 3, 2001).

26. Editorial, "Mr. Clinton's Legacy," *St. Louis Post-Dispatch* (August 16, 2000), p. B6.

27. Stephen Moore, quoted in John Ydstie, "Economic Legacy of President Bill Clinton," National Public Radio, *Morning Edition* (January 12, 2001). Historian Douglas Brinkley also argues that point, saying that Clinton was, at most, "sidestepping Congress" during that time. "I think he stole a lot of Republican thunder, which was smart." Brinkley, interviewed on Fox News, *The O'Reilly Factor* (December 27, 2000). The *Baltimore Sun* suggests that Clinton took a Republican idea, such as welfare reform, then made it his own with the earned-income credit rider. Editorial, "A Domestic Record of Progress, Pratfalls," *Baltimore Sun* (January 19, 2001), p. A28.

28. "I don't dislike the president, but I get a little tired, like Republicans do, about him taking credit for things for which he deserves no credit." John Kasich, Fox News, *The Edge with Paula Zahn* (January 9, 2001).

29. Philip Terzian, "In Search of a Legacy," Knight-Ridder/Tribune News Service (December 15, 2000); reprinted from the *Providence Journal*.

30. Editorial, "A Domestic Record of Progress, Pratfalls," *Baltimore Sun* (January 19, 2001), p. A28.

31. Editorial, "Oh Lucky Man: A Flawed President Finishes on a Positive Note," *Pittsburgh Post-Gazette* (January 20, 2001), p. A10.

32. Daniel Schorr, National Public Radio, *Weekend Edition* (June 28, 1997).

33. John Nielson, "Profile: Bill Clinton's Land Conservation Legacy," National Public Radio, *Morning Edition* (January 2, 2001).

34. Stephen Schier, quoted in Craig Gilbert, "Clinton's Legacy Begins to Form," *Milwaukee Journal-Sentinel* (January 16, 2001), p. 2.

35. Mara Liasson, "Clinton Legacy," National Public Radio, *Morning Edition* (January 1, 2001).

36. Jodi Evida, "Candidates Sharpen Their Stand-Up Skills," *The State* (Columbia, S.C.), (October 22, 2000), p. A19.

37. Steven Stark, National Public Radio, *Weekend Edition* (October 29, 2000).

38. Bob Edwards, National Public Radio, *Morning Edition* (January 4, 2001). Edwards was introducing John Ridley's piece, "Meeting with President Clinton Shows Him to be Regular Guy."

39. Quoted in Richard T. Cooper and Jack Nelson, "The 'Natural' Wraps Up His 8-Year Run," *Los Angeles Times* (January 14, 2001), p. A1.

40. Stephen J. Wayne, "Presidential Personality: The Clinton Legacy," in *The Clinton Scandal and the Future of American Government*, ed. Mark J. Rozell and Clyde Wilcox (Washington, DC: Georgetown University Press, 2000), p. 222.

41. See, for example, Associated Press, "Clinton's Legacy Plans Get in Democrats' Way," *St. Louis Post-Dispatch* (July 8, 1997), p. A4; and Ann McFeatters, "Clinton's Legacy Still in Limbo," *Denver Rocky Mountain News* (June 15, 1997), p. B5.

42. Dick Morris, *Behind the Oval Office: Winning the Presidency in the Nineties* (New York: Random House, 1997), p. 93.

43. In fact, Hitchens says, "[t]he Clinton years . . . have completed and locked in the Reagan revolution." Christopher Hitchens, "Bill of Goods?" *Mother Jones* 25 (September/October 2000), p. 55.

44. "He changed the image of the Democratic Party from a party of big spenders who were soft on crime to now a party that is the party of fiscal prudence and paying down the national debt." Mara Liasson, "Clinton Legacy," National Public Radio, *Morning Edition* (January 1, 2001).

45. George Watson, ABC News, *World News Now* (October 24, 2000). "The election of Bush may prove pivotal to Clinton's legacy. Had Gore won the White House, and especially had Democrats taken control of Congress, a number of initiatives Clinton proposed might have blossomed after his term, giving shape and definition to his presidency. As it is, eight years proved not enough for Clinton in many areas." Michael Hedges, "The Clinton Years: Legacy Viewed as Mixed," *Houston Chronicle* (January 14, 2001), p. A1.

46. Richard Cohen, "Frittering Away Clinton's Legacy," *Denver Post* (November 9, 2000), p. B11. For a thorough and fascinating account of the complicated, often tense relationship between Al Gore and Bill Clinton, see Marjorie Williams, "Scenes from a Marriage," *Vanity Fair* (July 2001), pp. 86–89, 132–37.

47. William Safire, "The Clothespin Vote," *New York Times* (November 6, 2000), p. A31. Safire went on to credit Clinton, however, for vetoing the "official secrets" bill. Many Americans evidently shared Safire's views: "About one in five voters said they chose Bush as a slap at Clinton." Richard Cohen, "Frittering Away Clinton's Legacy," *Denver Post* (November 9, 2000), p. B11.

48. See, for example, Bill Bennett's comment on NBC News, *Meet the Press* (January 14, 2001).

49. Richard Benedetto, "Clinton Must Do Something Bold to Achieve Greatness in History," *Gannett News Service* (November 13, 1999).

50. Michael Kazin, "Good Bill?" *Mother Jones* 25 (September/October 2000), p. 54.

51. Doris Kearns Goodwin, "What We'll Remember," *Time* 156 (November 20, 2000), p. 90.

52. Harvey Weinstein, "What We'll Remember," *Time* 156 (November 20, 2000), p. 90.

53. Douglas Brinkley, in ibid.

54. Christopher Hitchens, on CNBC, *Hardball* (January 18, 2001).

55. Dennis Miller, HBO, *Dennis Miller Live* (January 12, 2001).

56. For example, Edmund Morris, who has written biographies of Theodore Roosevelt and Ronald Reagan, referred to Clinton's "truck-driver values." Morris, "What We'll Remember," *Time* 156 (November 20, 2000), p. 90; Gail Collins, "Rudy's Next Stand," *New York Times* (January 26, 2001), p. A23.

57. Editorial, "Oh Lucky Man: A Flawed President Finishes on a Positive Note," *Pittsburgh Post-Gazette* (January 20, 2001), p. A10.

58. Robert Bartley, "What We'll Remember," *Time* 156 (November 20, 2000), p. 90.

59. Editorial, "Pardons on the Sly," *New York Times* (January 25, 2001), p. A26.

60. "Begging Pardons," *New York Times* (January 29, 2001), p. A1; "Mrs. Clinton's Unsteady Start," *New York Times* (February 1, 2001), p. A22; "Sorting Out the Pardon Mess," *New York Times* (February 23, 2001), p. A20.

61. James J. Pfiffner, "Presidential Character: Multidimensional or Seamless?" in *The Clinton Scandal and the Future of American Government*, ed. Mark J. Rozell and Clyde Wilcox (Washington, DC: Georgetown Univesity Press, 2000), p. 248.

62. Frank Newport, Gallup Poll Editor, interviewed on CNN, *Today* (December 20, 2000).

63. David W. Moore, "Good Times for Clinton as President, but Personal Reputation Hits New Low," *Gallup Poll Monthly* 400 (January 1999), p. 3.

64. Will then asked Schlesinger if he would like to "apologize" for having said previously that Ronald Reagan was not a great president. Schlesinger chuckled no.

65. James MacGregor Burns and Georgia Sorenson, *Dead Center* (1999).

66. David Kennedy, "Bill Clinton in the Eye of History," *New York Times* (November 2, 2000), p. A31.

67. Sean Wilentz, "Beyond Monica: The Future of Clinton's Past," *Nation* 267 (September 7, 1998), p. 13.

68. Marion Patch, in "Last Week We Asked: How Will Clinton's Presidency Be Recalled?" *Arizona Republic* (August 26, 2000), p. B6.

69. Akber A. Kassam, letter, *Milwaukee Journal-Sentinel* (January 13, 2001), p. A10.

70. Paul Greenberg, "Clinton's Legacy Will Be One of Political Disgrace," *Houston Chronicle* (November 3, 1996), p. 3; reprinted from *Little Rock Democrat Gazette*.

71. Christopher Hitchens, "Bill of Goods?" *Mother Jones* 25 (September/October 2000), p. 55.

72. This is the argument of Michael Kranish, "Impeachment, Contempt May Top Clinton Legacy," *Boston Globe* (April 14, 1999), p. A14.

73. Josh Getlin, "Clinton Legacy May Be History," *Los Angeles Times* (August 19, 1998), p. A16.

74. Mark Knoller, quoted in CBS News, *The Early Show*, "White House Correspondents Look Back on the Clinton Presidency" (January 18, 2001).

75. Michael Hedges, "The Clinton Years: Legacy Viewed as Mixed," *Houston Chronicle* (January 14, 2001), p. A1.

76. Richard T. Cooper and Jack Nelson, "The 'Natural' Wraps Up His 8-Year Run," *Los Angeles Times* (January 14, 2001), Part I, p. A1. Former Republican press secretary Marlin Fitzwater told Cooper and Nelson that Clinton "has an ability to connect with the common better than any politician I've known. . . . He's the best."

77. "I think he is going to be well remembered by the people at large. They will forgive him for the moral failures, by and large, and remember him for the progress. But I think historians will not remember him so well. Historians like milestones. They like major advances that they can point to, and they will see fewer of those and they will see the impeachment." David Gergen, from NBC News, *Meet the Press* (January 14, 2001).

78. David Gergen, NBC News, *Meet the Press* (January 14, 2001).

79. Douglas Brinkley, interviewed on Fox News, *The O'Reilly Factor* (December 27, 2000).

80. Terry Moe, quoted in Michael Hedges, "The Clinton Years: Legacy Viewed as Mixed," *Houston Chronicle* (January 14, 2001), p. A1.

81. Editorial, "A Domestic Record of Progress, Pratfalls," *Baltimore Sun* (January 19, 2001), p. A28.

82. "Last Week We Asked: How Will Clinton's Presidency Be Recalled?" *Arizona Republic* (August 26, 2000), p. B6.

83. Mara Liasson, "Profile: Efforts by President Clinton to Fill His Final Year in Office with Accomplishments," National Public Radio, *Morning Edition* (June 20, 2000).

84. Michael Armacost, quoted in Michael Hedges, "The Clinton Years: Legacy Viewed as Mixed," *Houston Chronicle* (January 14, 2001), p. A1.

85. R. Emmett Tyrrell, Jr., "The Clinton Legacy: A Scherzo," *American Spectator* 33 (September 2000), p. 14.

86. Ed Rollins, interview, CNN, *Inside Politics* (May 28, 1997).

87. Editorial, "Mr. Clinton's Legacy," *St. Louis Post-Dispatch* (August 16, 2000), p. B6.

88. Rev. Peter J. Gomes, "What We'll Remember," *Time* 156 (November 20, 2000), p. 90.

89. Safire, "Clinton Divides Jerusalem," *New York Times* (January 4, 2001), p. A25.

For Further Reading

Abrams, Floyd. "Clinton Versus the First Amendment." *New York Times*. March 30, 1997, VI, p. 42.

Anonymous. [Joe Klein]. *Primary Colors: A Novel of Politics*. New York: Random House, 1996.

"Beyond Monica: The Future of Clinton's Past." *The Nation*. September 7, 1998, p. 11.

Brill, Steven. "Pressgate." *Brill's Content*. July/August 1998, p. 13.

Cannon, Carl. "A Flack Who Uses a Smile." *Baltimore Sun*. May 19, 1996, p. E1.

Denton, Robert E., Jr., ed. *The 1996 Presidential Campaign: A Communication Perspective*. Westport, CT: Praeger Publishers, 1998.

Denton, Robert E., Jr., and Rachel L. Holloway, eds. *The Clinton Presidency: Images, Issues, and Communication Strategies*. Westport, CT: Praeger Publishers, 1996.

Dershowitz, Alan M. *Sexual McCarthyism: Clinton, Starr, and the Emerging Constitutional Crisis*. New York: Basic Books, 1998.

FitzSimon, Martha, ed. *Covering the Presidential Primaries*. New York: Freedom Forum Media Studies Center, June 1992.

———. *The Finish Line: Covering the Campaign's Final Days*. New York: Freedom Forum Media Studies Center, January 1993.

———. *An Uncertain Season: Reporting in the Postprimary Period*. New York: Freedom Forum Media Studies Center, September 1992.

FitzSimon, Martha, and Edward C. Pease, eds. *The Homestretch: New Politics.*

New Media. New Voters? New York: Freedom Forum Media Studies Center, October 1992.

Foster, Donald. "Primary Culprit." *New York.* February 26, 1996, pp. 50–57.

Gartner, Michael. "How the Monica Story Played in Mid-America." *Columbia Journalism Review.* May/June 1999, p. 34.

Graham, Tim. *Pattern of Deception: The Media's Rule in the Clinton Presidency.* Alexandria, VA: Media Research Center, 1996.

Grove, Lloyd. "The White House Kiddie Corps." *Washington Post.* June 1, 1993, p. C1.

Hanson, Christopher. "How to Satisfy a Spin-ster Every Time." *Columbia Journalism Review.* July/August 1993, p. 17.

Hart, Roderick P. *Campaign Talk: Why Elections Are Good For Us.* Princeton, NJ: Princeton University Press, 2000.

Hitchens, Christopher. *No One Left to Lie to: The Triangulations of William Jefferson Clinton.* London: Verso, 1999.

"Hollywood Inspired by Clinton Era." *Milwaukee Journal.* November 4, 2000, p. B6.

Jubera, Drew. "Campaign '96: The Candidate Talk Show Built." *Atlanta Journal-Constitution.* February 24, 1996, p. A10.

Kennedy, David. "Bill Clinton in the Eye of History." *New York Times.* November 2, 2000, p. A31.

Klein, Joe. "The Bill Clinton Show." *Newsweek.* October 26, 1992, p. 35.

Kurtz, Howard. *Media Circus: The Trouble with America's Newspapers.* New York: Times Books, 1993.

———. *Spin Cycle: Inside the Clinton Propaganda Machine.* New York: Free Press, 1998.

Lambrecht, Bill. "Polls Can Drive Campaign Tactics, Voter Perceptions." *St. Louis Post-Dispatch.* October 27, 1996, p. 24.

Levinson, Barry. "Hey, We Were Just Kidding." *Newsweek.* February 9, 1998, p. 51.

Lull, James, and Stephen Hinerman, eds. *Media Scandals: Morality and Desire in the Popular Culture Marketplace.* New York: Columbia University Press, 1997.

Maraniss, David. *First in His Class: A Biography of Bill Clinton.* New York: Simon & Schuster, 1995.

Meeropol, Michael. *Surrender: How the Clinton Administration Completed the Reagan Revolution.* Ann Arbor: University of Michigan Press, 1998.

Ostrow, Joanne. "Clinton Media Dissected." *Denver Post.* February 22, 1999, p. E5.

Page, Benjamin I., ed. *Crosstalk: Citizens, Candidates, and the Media in a Presidential Campaign.* Chicago: University of Chicago Press, 1996.

Patterson, Thomas E. *Out of Order.* New York: Alfred A. Knopf, 1993.

Pomper, Gerald M., ed. *The Election of 1992: Reports and Interpretations.* Chatham, NJ: Chatham House Publishers, 1993.

———. *The Election of 1996: Reports and Interpretations.* Chatham, NJ: Chatham House Publishers, 1997.

Rodriguez, Juan. "The Power of Blather." *Montreal Gazette.* February 8, 1998, p. D1.

Rosenstiel, Tom. *Strange Bedfellows: How Television and the Presidential Candidates Changed American Politics, 1992.* New York: Hyperion, 1993.

Rozell, Mark J., and Clyde Wilcox, eds. *The Clinton Scandal and the Future of American Government.* Washington, D.C.: Georgetown University Press, 2000.

Safire, William. "Blizzard of Lies." *New York Times.* January 8, 1996, p. A27.

Shogren, Elizabeth. "Spinmeister McCurry Leaving the Podium." *Los Angeles Times.* July 24, 1998, p. A22.

Smith, Stephen A., ed. *Bill Clinton on Stump, State, and Stage: The Rhetorical Road to the White House.* Fayetteville: University of Arkansas Press, 1994.

Starobin, Paul. "A Generation of Vipers." *Columbia Journalism Review.* November/December 1994, p. 42.

Stephanopoulos, George. *All Too Human: A Political Education.* Boston: Little, Brown and Co., 1999.

Stewart, James B. *Blood Sport: The President and His Adversaries.* New York: Simon & Schuster, 1996.

Thomas, Evan, with Michael Isikoff. "Clinton Versus Paula Jones." *Newsweek.* January 13, 1997, p. 26.

Von Drehle, David. "Bill Clinton's Movers and Shapers." *Washington Post.* March 23, 1992, p. D1.

Branegan, Jay. "What We'll Remember." *Time.* November 20, 2000, p. 90.

Witcover, Jules. "Where We Went Wrong." *Columbia Journalism Review.* March/April 1998, p. 19.

Woodward, Bob. *The Agenda: Inside the Clinton White House.* New York: Simon & Schuster, 1994.

———. *Shadow: Five Presidents and the Legacy of Watergate.* New York: Simon & Schuster, 1999.

Wright, Russell O. *Presidential Elections in the United States: A Statistical History, 1860–1992.* Jefferson, North Carolina: McFarland & Co., 1995.

Index

About the Author

JOSEPH HAYDEN is a freelance writer and former journalist.

DATE DUE

JUL 0 6 2004			
GAYLORD			PRINTED IN U.S.A.